T0350015

1915 *Diary of* S. An-sky

From left to right: Abram Rekhtman, Solomon Iudovin, S. An-sky, Sholem Aleichem,
Olga Rabinovich, M. A. Ginzburg. © "Petersburg Judaica."

1915 DIARY OF

S. An-sky

A RUSSIAN

JEWISH

WRITER

at the

EASTERN

FRONT

S. A. An-sky

Translated from the Russian and with an
Introduction by Polly Zavadivker

INDIANA UNIVERSITY PRESS   *Bloomington & Indianapolis*

This book is a publication of

INDIANA UNIVERSITY PRESS
Office of Scholarly Publishing
Herman B. Wells Library 350
1320 East 10th Street
Bloomington, Indiana 47405 USA

iupress.indiana.edu

*Manufactured in the
United States of America*

Cataloging information is available
from the Library of Congress.

ISBN 978-0-253-02045-1 (cloth)
ISBN 978-0-253-02053-6 (ebook)

1 2 3 4 5   21 20 19 18 17 16

For

JEFFREY

Contents

Acknowledgments   *ix*

Note on Translation   *xi*

INTRODUCTION   *1*

S. An-sky's 1915 Diary

1   WINTER 1915: *Galicia*   *39*

2   FALL 1915: *Petrograd*   *129*

Notes   *159*

Index   *183*

Acknowledgments

IT IS AN HONOR TO THANK THOSE WHO HAVE HELPED TO TRANS-form a long lost archival document into a book that bears An-sky's name.

I am deeply grateful to Gabriella Safran, who shared her own copy of the archival diary with me and enthusiastically encouraged the work of translating it into English. My profound thanks to Carol Avins for her comments on my first draft of the translation and for the several sources she shared from her previous research on Isaac Babel's war diary. As my graduate adviser and mentor, Nathaniel Deutsch provided critical insights and intellectual inspiration at every stage of this project.

The Introduction and diary translation were greatly improved by reviews from Eugene Avrutin and an anonymous reader for Indiana University Press. Sibelan Forrester generously provided feedback that strengthened the translation, as did Yuri Radchenko and Robert Chandler. Sam Casper, Gennady Estraikh, Kiril Feferman, Victoria Khiterer, Joshua Shanes, Dmitry Tartakovsky, and Arkadii Zeltser kindly responded to my inquiries and assisted my search for information in various archives and libraries.

The photographs included in this book were located with the help of archivists and librarians in Ukraine, Poland, the United States, and Israel. I thank Bohdan Shumylovych at the Center for Urban History of

East Central Europe in Lviv, Sylwia Zawacka at the National Digital Archive in Warsaw, Vital Zajka at the YIVO Institute for Jewish Research in New York, and Michael Simonson at the Leo Baeck Institute in New York. From Israel, Natasha Ratner sent me family photographs of Boris Ratner, and Tami Hausner Raveh shared with me photographs of her grandfather Bernard Hausner.

I thank Janet Rabinovitch and Robert Sloan, former directors at Indiana University Press, who supported this publication in its initial stages. It has been a privilege to work with Dee Mortensen, Janice Frisch, Mikala Guyton, and Karen Hallman while preparing the manuscript.

Research for the introduction and annotations were completed with the assistance of the Professor Bernard Choseed Memorial Fellowship at the YIVO Institute for Jewish Research, and the Dr. Sophie Bookhalter Fellowship in Jewish Culture at the Center for Jewish History in New York. I also extend thanks to my colleagues at the University of Delaware for helping to create the productive atmosphere in which I have been able to teach and write for the past two years.

This translation is dedicated to my husband Jeffrey Berman, for always drawing me out of the rubble.

Note on Translation

THIS TRANSLATION IS BASED UPON TWO SURVIVING FRAG-
ments of An-sky's war diary, now held at the Russian State Archive of
Literature and Art in Moscow. The first section was written between
January 1 and March 8, 1915, and the second between September 9 and
October 10, 1915.

An-sky wrote his diary in Russian, but he frequently used Yiddish
and Hebrew in his daily interactions as well as his diary entries. His
diary also contains occasional phrases in German, Polish, French, and
other languages. This translation seeks to preserve the multilingual tex-
ture of the original by presenting foreign terms and expressions in ital-
ics. Readers will find explanations of all foreign terms in the notes.

Yiddish terms are transliterated here according to the YIVO classifi-
cation system. Russian and Hebrew words are transliterated according
to the Library of Congress system, although diacritical marks have been
omitted, and exceptions have been made for names that have gained common spellings in English (e.g., Gorky, rather than Gor'kii; Jabotinsky, rather than Zhabotinskii). The spelling of some Russian names has also been
modified in order to facilitate pronunciation (e.g., Fyodor, not Fedor).

Place-names used in the diary refer to locations that were then part
of the Austro-Hungarian and Russian Empires and are found in today's

Russia, Lithuania, Poland, Belarus, and Ukraine. An-sky's Russian spellings have been retained for locations that were then part of the Russian Empire and eastern Galicia. Names of locations then part of western Galicia (found in today's Poland) are given with Polish spellings.

An-sky's dates for his diary entries were given according to the Julian calendar, which fell thirteen days behind the Gregorian calendar and was used in Russia until January 1918.

1915 *Diary of* S. An-sky

Introduction

THE FIRST-EVER PUBLICATION AND TRANSLATION OF S. AN-SKY'S
diary from 1915 bring to light a remarkable personal account of a water-
shed era in Russian, Jewish, and East European history. It is a document
whose author was both a critical witness to history and a fascinating
figure in his own right. An-sky, pseudonym of Shloyme Zanvil Rapoport
(1863–1920) was a Russian Jewish writer, ethnographer, and revolutionary, best known today for his play *The Dybbuk*, one of the most widely
performed works of Jewish theater in the world. In a Russian-language
diary that he kept throughout the First World War, An-sky chronicled
his experiences working for the Jewish Committee for the Aid of War
Victims, an organization known by its Russian acronym as EKOPO.[1] As
an aid worker for EKOPO, An-sky played an important role in what was
the largest relief campaign ever undertaken in Jewish history to that
date—an immense coordinated initiative to assist tens of thousands of
refugees as well as victims of mass expulsions that were carried out by
the Russian Army during the first year of the war.

An-sky's aid work among Jewish civilians brought him to Galicia and
Bukovina, provinces of the Austro-Hungarian Empire that the Russian
Army occupied twice during the war, first in 1914–1915, and again in
1916–1917. Inhabited mainly by Poles, Ukrainians, and Jews, Galicia and

FIGURE 0.1. An-sky wearing the uniform of a Russian aid worker, including wool hat with a Red Cross insignia, an armband, and a wool-lined vest. *Gezamelte shriftn in fuftsen bender*, 15 vols. (Vilna: Farlag "An-sky," 1920–1925), 4: frontispiece.

Bukovina experienced some of the war's most devastating violence, and Jews suffered a particularly harsh fate at the hands of the Russian occupying powers. These territories, which are today divided between southeastern Poland, western Ukraine, and northeast Romania, formed part of what is now known as the Eastern Front of the First World War.

Although An-sky kept a diary throughout the war, only fragments of it have survived, namely four months of entries that were written from January to March and September to October 1915. The publication of his diary a century later makes a rare source available for the first time—what is currently the only English-language eyewitness account from a Jewish writer who saw the Russian side of the Eastern Front.[2] With this volume, An-sky's war diary also joins the growing number of eyewitness sources available in English about the long-neglected subject of Russia's Great War.[3] But while many of the available firsthand sources were penned by high-ranking Russian military figures and politicians, An-sky's diary reflects the unique perspective of a revolutionary writer, a relief worker among war victims, and a Jewish nationalist.

An-sky was well known as a Russian and Yiddish writer among his contemporaries, and his diary is very much a writer's diary. It stands out for its striking literary quality, the memorable stories of military and civilian life that it tells, and its keen observations about the impact of war on daily life and human civilization. An-sky did not dwell on his own thoughts or emotions at length, but rather, was an avid observer of his surroundings, always writing as if he were standing in the eye of a storm. As a diarist, he sought to capture the images, sounds, and landscape of war. Among the many people he met during his travels throughout the war zone, those who fascinated him the most were ordinary Jewish men and women, whose stories he diligently recorded in his diary.

Fifty-one years old when the war broke out, An-sky had spent the three previous decades of his life engaged in cultural and political work among both Jews and Russians. A charismatic and energetic organizer, he devoted his talents to a variety of social causes during the war, including aid work, Jewish cultural nationalism, and Russian revolutionary politics. An-sky's protean interests led him to a wide range of places in wartime Russia. His diary allows readers to glimpse the inside of military hospitals, train stations, jail cells, and devastated synagogues in Russian-occupied Galicia, and theaters, homes of wealthy philanthropists, and publishing houses in Kiev, Moscow, and Petrograd. Through An-sky's eyes, we see a cross-section of Russian society, the home front and front zone, both reeling from the impact of a catastrophic war from which the empire will not emerge intact.

In addition to his work as a writer, An-sky also had years of experience as an ethnographer of East European Jewry. Between 1912 and 1914, he led a "Jewish Ethnographic Expedition" to collect folklore in the Russian Empire's Pale of Settlement (in Russian, *cherta osedlosti*), the vast region between the Baltic and Black Seas where nearly five million Jews, or over 90 percent of the empire's Jewish population, lived within delineated borders by legal decree until 1917.[4] An-sky carried out the expedition under the auspices of the Jewish Historical-Ethnographic Society in Saint Petersburg, a scholarly organization founded in 1908, with a groundbreaking mission to study and preserve Jewish history, especially that of Jews in the Pale of Settlement. During the expedition An-sky and his ambitious team of folklorists toured the provinces of Volynia and Podolia, in the southwestern Pale (part of right-bank Ukraine), passing through some sixty towns where Jews, and Hasidic communities in particular, composed a significant segment of the population.[5] In these towns (known in Yiddish as *shtetlakh*, and in Russian as *mestechki*), An-sky's team transcribed and recorded hundreds of songs, stories, and parables; photographed synagogues, tombstones, and cemeteries; and collected both sacred and everyday objects, ranging from Torah scrolls to women's headdresses and medicinal folk remedies. An-sky viewed these materials as emblems of the rich, but little-known cultural heritage of East European Jewry. He believed that with exposure to new audiences—modern, secular Jews in particular—these objects could be given new life, whether as content for museum displays, or inspiration for artistic works such as plays and paintings. But he was equally concerned, too, that the traditional Jewish folk culture of small-town Jews—"an inheritance," as he put it, "from hundreds of generations of the chosen"—would vanish and be lost to historical memory, if not carefully documented and preserved: "With every old man who dies, with every small-town fire, with every exile," he wrote, "a piece of our past is lost, and the most beautiful expressions of traditional life . . . disappear."[6]

After the outbreak of war in July 1914, the prospects of death, fire, and exile that initially compelled An-sky to document shtetl life loomed larger than ever and, indeed, threatened the very parts of the Russian Empire where he had been tirelessly collecting folklore since 1912. Assisting Jewish war victims was an imperative in its own right, and also provided An-sky a means to continue his campaign to preserve national and cultural treasures, precisely at a time when they were most threatened.

An-sky also viewed his war diary as part of a larger movement to create and preserve records of the Jewish experience of a significant historical event. Like many other intellectuals of his time, he wanted to write a testimony, to leave his account of having confronted and survived a colossal and transformative period of history.[7] Although An-sky's immediate goal as an aid worker was to assist Jewish war victims in the present, he also intended for his diary and wartime writings to serve a practical purpose in the future. In an "Appeal" cowritten with Yiddish writers I. L. Peretz and Yankev Dinezon, and published in January 1915 in the daily newspaper *Haynt* (Today), An-sky called on Jews to write down and collect accounts of their wartime experiences—and especially, of their hardships:

> Each drop of our shed blood, each tear, each act of suffering and sacrifice must be entered into our historical account. Whoever sows blood has the right to reap! We must become the historians of our part in the process. . . . Record everything, knowing thereby that you are collecting useful and necessary material for the reconstruction of Jewish history.[8]

Like many other observers of the Great War, An-sky, Dinezon, and Peretz expected that the borders of Eastern Europe would drastically change after the war. As future members of nations that would be created as a result of the war, it was incumbent upon Jews to record their wartime history, for it was believed that on the basis of that history— the blood and tears they had shed during the war—they could justify their demands for political rights and material resources in those new nations. It was therefore critically important that Jews assume responsibility for writing their own history.

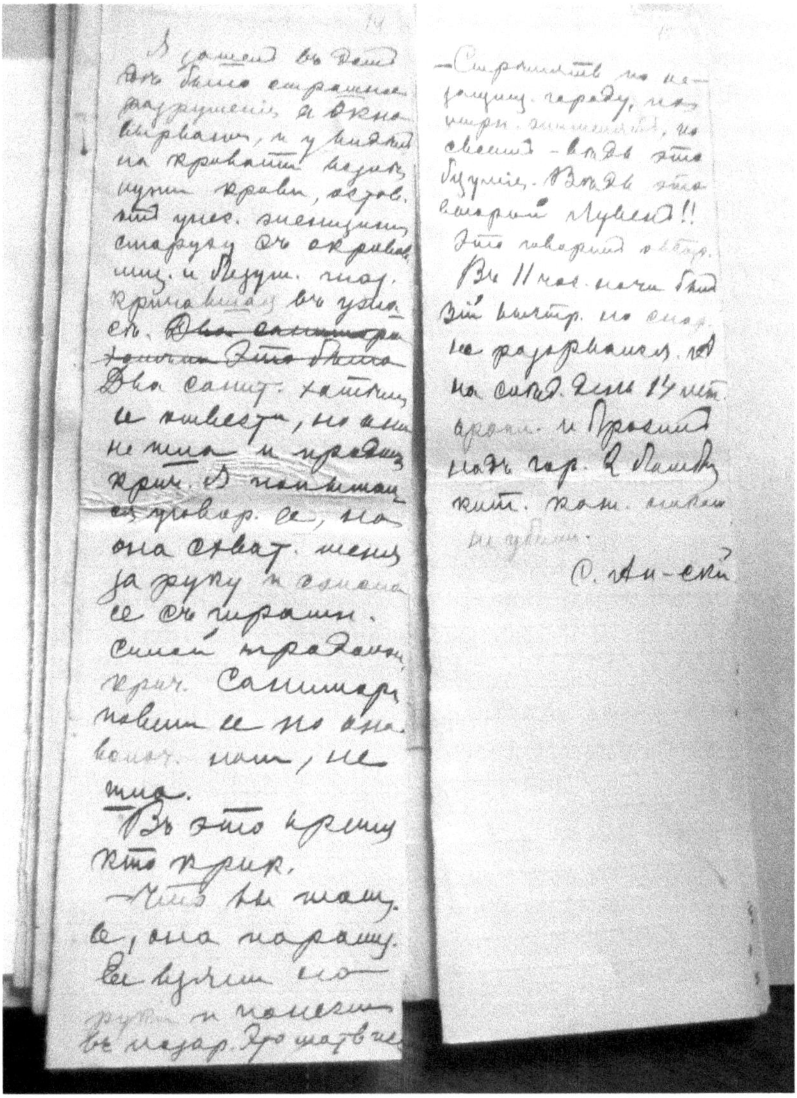

FIGURE 0.2. An-sky's notes from February 14, 1915. These notes were not part of his diary but were recorded in a separate notebook, in which he wrote multiple versions of events that took place on February 14, 1915. Judaica Section, Manuscript Division, Vernadsky National Library of Ukraine, Kiev. *Photograph by Polly Zavadivker.*

An-sky, Dinezon, and Peretz exhorted their readers to help build a national archive of Jewish wartime suffering, as it were, and An-sky's own diary can be understood as a contribution to that effort. Indeed, his own archival impulse extended far beyond writing a diary, to the collection of any and all documentary material he could get his hands on. By the end of the war, An-sky had amassed a vast personal archive: 1,371 war-related documents, including letters from fellow relief workers, eyewitness descriptions of pogroms, copies of military decrees and circulars, travel documents, death sentence reports, and much more.[9]

While An-sky's compulsion to collect was perhaps extreme, it also expressed a widely shared cultural value among Jews in Russia at the time. In 1915, the Jewish Historical-Ethnographic Society issued its own appeal for Jews to send documents and objects to its museum for safekeeping; also in 1915, Russian Jewish political activists collected enough documents about Russian military atrocities to fill five published volumes.[10] A number of great thinkers of An-sky's generation, including the historian Simon Dubnov and poet Chaim Nachman Bialik, regarded their own diaries, correspondence, and autobiographical statements in a similar fashion, as documents to be entered into the archives of Jewish national history.[11] The exhaustively detailed nature of An-sky's diary suggests that he too reflected on the significance of his life and experiences of the war with this aim in mind.

An-sky's eyewitness account of the war became a first, and not only, description of his wartime experiences. During the revolution that followed Russia's Great War, he fled from the country and left his war diary behind at the time. An-sky left Russia because the Socialist Revolutionary (SR) party, of which he was a prominent member, came under attack by the Bolsheviks, following the attempt of an SR activist on Lenin's life in Moscow on August 30, 1918. An-sky, who was laying low in Moscow at the time, decided to leave the city when the Cheka (Bolshevik Secret Police) began to hunt down and round up SRs as part of the Red Terror. He traveled west and resettled in Vilna, then under German control.[12]

An-sky escaped Russia with his life, but never managed to recover an entire copy of his diary. Through unknown circumstances, two parts of his diary were brought to Russia's central literary archive, where they have remained to this day.[13] These two fragments contained the nearly four months of diary entries upon which this translation is based.

Although An-sky abandoned his war diary in Moscow, he succeeded in making some of its contents known to the world. During and after the war, he revised parts of his war diary as a memoir, and during the process of revision, An-sky also translated his war diary from Russian into Yiddish. He completed the first section of his Yiddish memoir by April 1918, and finished three more sections nearly two years later, in February 1920.[14] A composition in four parts that ran to more than six hundred pages, it was the longest work he had ever written. The title of his memoir—*The Jewish Destruction of Poland, Galicia and Bukovina, from a Diary, 1914–1917*—also revealed that a diary had been its original source.[15]

As An-sky's war diaries began to gather dust in Moscow, his Yiddish memoir, commonly referred to as *The Destruction of Galicia* (in Yiddish, *Khurbn Galitsye*), went on to become one of his best-known literary works. In the early 1920s, it was printed in a three-volume Yiddish version, the first volume of which corresponded to the diaries he had left behind in Moscow. In 1929, a Hebrew translation was published in Berlin.[16] Most recently, an abridged English translation appeared in 2002.[17] The English-language publication helped to strengthen a renewal of scholarly and public interest in both An-sky himself, as well as Russia's own long-eclipsed history of the Great War.[18] An-sky's insightful portrayals of military and civilian life have subsequently appeared in a range of scholarship about the Russian, Jewish, and East European experience of World War I.[19] It is regarded as a magisterial historical epic, a tragic and heroic narrative known for its impassioned moral convictions, and perceptive analyses of the wartime fate of East European Jews. *The Destruction of Galicia* has also become an iconic text in Jewish cultural memory, a work that embodies the tradition of documenting catastrophic events in the Jewish past.[20]

The publication here of the surviving fragments of An-sky's diary from 1915 reveals the raw material that served as his basis for *The Destruction of Galicia*. Readers will also find much in the diary that never appeared in *The Destruction of Galicia*. Of the four months of diary entries that are published here, An-sky in fact chose not to include more than half in his memoir, including the first three weeks of January 1915, and all of September and October 1915.

The differences between the content of the unpublished diary and the published memoir can be explained by the author's intentions. An-sky wrote *The Destruction of Galicia* during the years that followed the war in order to present a moral and artistic vision of the war. As he contemplated and wrote about his experiences in hindsight, he sought to create a coherent story, a narrative of lyrical pathos. The story revolved around a central figure—a heroic, lone aid worker on a desperate and solitary mission to save a tribe of Jews from total destruction. The diary entries present a rather different story, and An-sky was selective in what he chose to incorporate from the unedited and firsthand impressions contained in them. In contrast to his memoir, An-sky's language in the diary, which is stark, fragmentary, and often elliptical, mirrors the starts and stops of everyday life in a time of war. It brings us as close as we can possibly come to An-sky's experience of reality. We follow him as he navigates unexpected turns of daily life in a front zone—his immediate reactions to a devastating bombing in Tarnów, a desperate search for lost train cars in Radivilov, and his repeated discoveries in virtually every city and shtetl of scarcity, hunger, and desperation among Jews.

Whereas in retrospect An-sky had time to contemplate the violence of war, his diary entries conveyed a sense of shock. Unprepared for the horrors that he confronted in the war zone, An-sky often expressed vulnerability, frustration, anxiety, and a sense of powerlessness to comprehend or alleviate the human suffering that he witnessed. Driven by a powerful sense of obligation to help Jewish war victims, but often lacking the means to do anything but listen and observe, An-sky's recourse, as a diarist, was to "record everything," as he had written in the "Appeal"— to capture as much as possible of the events, personalities, conversations, and stories he heard, knowing all the while that this could serve him as "useful and necessary material for the reconstruction of Jewish history." Writing may have served An-sky as a means to capture, preserve, and relate a terrible reality that he was otherwise powerless to alter.

The recovery of An-sky's unpublished war diary therefore presents us with a fascinating opportunity to trace a writer's personal journey through a catastrophic era of history, from his first iteration of events in his diary to the epic historical narrative into which it was transformed. An-sky's diary was not merely a first draft of history, but should also be read as a distinct documentary source in its own right. A discussion of the wartime and revolutionary context in which he composed his 1915 diary, to which we now turn, can shed light on its historical and literary significance.

HOME FRONT AND WAR FRONT: RELIEF
WORK IN WARTIME RUSSIA

Russia entered the world war against the Central Powers on July 19, 1914. In the days that followed, the Russian Army mobilized four million troops along a two-thousand mile long front—a Northwest Front against Germany, and Southwest Front against Austria-Hungary.[21] The outbreak of war upended civilian life in the Russian Empire as well. On August 18, Saint Petersburg was renamed Petrograd, so as to sound more patriotically Slavic and less German; and a tsarist decree placed territories west of Petrograd under martial law, allowing for military control of censorship and all aspects of civilian life.[22] Petrograd, along with large parts of the empire's interior, became part of the Russian "home front."

An-sky was living in Petrograd when the war began. With a population of nearly thirty-five thousand Jews, the city was home to some of Russia's most important Jewish intellectuals, financial elites, and institutions.[23] Although these institutions' headquarters were located in the empire's capital and managed by Petrograd Jewry, they had been founded with the goal to improve the social, cultural, and material welfare of the Jewish masses in the Pale of Settlement. They sponsored networks of Russian and Yiddish-language schools, theaters, and libraries; published innovative scholarship and journalism; and employed physicians and ran clinics and sanatoria throughout the empire.[24]

Petrograd was part of the Russian home front, but the vast majority of Russian Jews, those in the Pale of Settlement, now found themselves living in what had become a war zone—the territory where the Russian Army's Northwest and Southwest Fronts had been established. Although Jews in Petrograd found themselves hundreds of miles to the east of the front zone, they immediately began to mobilize the existing organizations doing cultural, educational, and medical work in the region to serve the needs of Jewish soldiers and war victims.

The first step to form a coordinated wartime relief campaign was taken in Petrograd on August 18, 1914, when a group of Russian-Jewish bankers, lawyers, and philanthropists founded EKOPO, the official Relief Committee of Russian Jewry (An-sky referred to EKOPO throughout his diary simply as "the Committee," or "Relief Committee"). Over the next four years, EKOPO established branches throughout the Russian Empire and provided hundreds of thousands of Jewish war victims with food, medicine, transportation, loans and credit, legal aid, schools for children and adults, job placement, and vocational training.[25] As an officially authorized organization, and with a budget of thirty-one million rubles—a vast sum for the time—EKOPO became the single most powerful Jewish organization in Russia during the war. The Russian government provided more than half of its income, and the remainder came from prominent patrons such as the Gintsburg family, as well as philanthropic organizations in the West, most notably the American Jewish Joint Distribution Committee.

EKOPO developed into a large and influential aid organization due to highly inauspicious circumstances. Jews in wartime Russia experienced unprecedented forms of hardship and violence during the war. By November 1914, nearly six million Jews throughout Eastern Europe—well over half of the world's Jewish population at the time—found themselves living under Russian martial law, including five million in the Russian Empire, and one million in occupied Galicia and Bukovina. Russian military violence targeted entire communities, and the worst episodes took place in late 1914 and 1915. The immediate trigger of the violence was spy mania—a phenomenon that swept virtually every belligerent country, but which the Russian Army in particular expressed through a ferocious and systematic persecution of the Jews living under its authority.[26] To be sure, many minorities living within Russia's borders—especially Germans, but also Poles, Latvians, Muslims,

Chinese, and others—came under suspicion as potential fifth columns. But tales of Jewish espionage were extraordinarily elaborate, widely circulated, and had devastating consequences for Jewish civilian populations. Military commanders at the highest echelons espoused the idea that the Jew was an "internal enemy." The Army's Commander in Chief Nikolai Nikolaevich, and Chief of Staff Nikolai Ianushkevich both bluntly declared that every Jew in Russian territory was actively aiding the German Army.[27] Their views spread to officers, troops, and local populations alike and gave tacit sanction to a widespread understanding that army violence against Jewish civilians and property—robbery, wreckage, expulsion, extortion, rape, and even murder—was permissible.[28]

By August 1914, Russian military hostility toward Jews had manifested on multiple fronts with devastating force. The German Army routed Russia's First and Second Armies in a series of battles in Eastern Prussia that month. While retreating across north-central Poland, Russian forces expelled Jewish civilians in the region, sending a population of nearly eighty thousand poor and traumatized refugees to Warsaw. The shock of these initial expulsions was rapidly eclipsed by the violence that followed when the Russian Army invaded Galicia and Bukovina on August 7, 1914.

Galicia and Bukovina were rural and impoverished Habsburg provinces, home to nearly one million Jews, as well as 7.7 million Poles and Ruthenians (the name for Galicia's Slavic population before their adoption of "Ukrainian" as a term of self-description).[29] A swift Russian advance across Galicia sent hundreds of thousands of inhabitants fleeing west for safer parts of the Habsburg Empire, including as many as two hundred thousand Jews.[30] Between August and November, the Russians gained control of the entire province.[31] Under Russian military occupation, Jews in Galicia fell victim to a battery of abuses and humiliations, including mass arrest, deportation, forced labor, public beatings, murder, robbery, destruction of homes, and desecration of synagogues.

Back in Petrograd, An-sky and fellow Jewish leaders grew increasingly alarmed from reports about the conduct of the Russian military in Galicia, which appeared in Russian liberal newspapers, as well as

FIGURE 0.3. First patrol of Cossack forces in Lvov, September 3, 1914. Ihor Kotlobulatov Collection. *Courtesy of the Center for Urban History of East Central Europe, L'viv.*

eyewitness accounts from wounded soldiers who had been evacuated from the front.[32] As news of military atrocities in occupied Galicia filtered back to Petrograd, An-sky embarked on an attempt to aid Jewish civilians in other parts of the empire. He traveled to various cities where war victims had fled, gathered information about their critical needs, tried to organize help, and reported on his findings in articles for the Russian press. In October 1914, he traveled to Minsk, where he met scores of homeless Jewish refugees and sought to secure shelter for them by interceding with local municipal authorities.[33] That same month he visited Kiev, where he organized a large clothing drive. In November, he passed through Moscow, where he talked with wounded, grief-stricken soldiers at a Jewish hospital who had recently returned from Galicia.[34]

Following these initial forays into relief work, An-sky made more ambitious plans by setting out to help Jews living under Russian occupation in Galicia. When EKOPO's leaders learned of his intentions, they reached out to him with a proposal. On November 20, 1914, the organization's director Genrikh Sliozberg, and secretary L. M. Bramson wrote An-sky asking him to sign on as an official EKOPO plenipotentiary, or agent.[35] He would travel to Galicia, collect detailed facts about the conditions of Jews there, and establish connections with local relief committees that would then distribute aid on behalf of EKOPO. An-sky agreed. The next day he began to tackle his first major obstacle: securing entry as a civilian to Galicia, a highly restricted occupation zone.

An-sky's plan to get to Galicia involved taking on a second assignment, as an employee of either the Union of Zemstvos (VZS) or Union of Towns (VSG).[36] These organizations, which operated under the banner of the Red Cross, worked closely with military authorities to supply soldiers with much-needed medical treatment and supplies.[37] They also had official authorization from the Russian military to work in occupied Galicia. Yet although the unions were large organizations that employed over 230,000 workers, An-sky's prospects of securing employment with a division seemed slim. Although many union divisions were managed by liberal Russians (many of them members of the Constitutional Democrat, or Kadet Party), some prominent Russian military authorities—among them General Nikolai Ivanov, commander of the Southwest Front in Galicia—had made it known they felt the number of Jews employed in the vzs and vsG was too high and ought to be reduced.[38]

But An-sky knew that the vzs and vsG were the only organizations through which he would be able to obtain entry papers to Galicia. And so on November 21, the day after he received the letter from Sliozberg and Bramson, he left Petrograd for Warsaw, where several union divisions had their headquarters. In Warsaw he spent over a month making appeals, unsuccessfully, to various vzs and vsG division leaders for an assignment in Galicia. Still lacking official travel documents in late December, he reached Rovno, a city in Russia's Volynia province about sixty miles east of the border with Galicia. It is in Rovno, on January 1, 1915, that the first entry of the first surviving fragment of his diary begins, dropping us in medias res of his quest to enter Galicia.

"The new year was born in profound melancholy," he wrote on January 1. "Neither desires nor hopes, as though you were standing before a corpse." Not one to dwell on feelings of mortality or despair, An-sky moved on to describe his activities that day: he saw a "senseless" Yiddish play at a local theater where the "least talented of talentless actors performed"; visited a military hospital, where he sympathized with soldiers suffering from agonizing wounds; and made connections with locals who could potentially help him to reach Galicia.

Two days later, on January 3, An-sky reported on a breakthrough: a telegram from a Moscow friend, the industrialist and Zionist activist Yitzhak Naidich, informing him that a vzs division in Galicia led by one Igor Platonovich Demidov had an opening in the unit. As he learned after rushing back to Moscow that same day, Demidov was a Kadet deputy to the State Duma who ran a military hospital in the city of Tarnów, directly behind the Russian front line in western Galicia (throughout his diary An-sky referred to the hospital as the State Duma Hospital). Demidov needed An-sky to deliver a shipment of linens and medicine from Moscow to Tarnów. In one direction alone, the journey by train was almost 1,600 kilometers (1,000 miles) in length. An-sky would depart from Moscow with the train cars, move them south to Kiev, then east across Galicia via Brody and Lvov. An-sky's task would not be easy: winter had brought freezing temperatures and snow, and the rail lines to and from Galicia were badly congested with trains carrying troops and weapons, which were given priority over medical supplies. But most importantly, the journey would allow him the opportunity to traverse Galicia from east to west, thus providing chances to visit dozens of Jewish communities in shtetls and cities along the way.

An-sky prepared for an immediate departure to Galicia, but first made brief stops in Moscow, Petrograd, and Kiev, where he informed local EKOPO committees about the purpose of his upcoming trip, and raised thousands of rubles for Galician Jewry. On January 12, he left Moscow for Tarnów, traveling with a young, socialist Jewish lawyer named Boris Ratner, who had volunteered with Demidov's unit out of sheer curiosity to visit Russian-occupied Galicia.

In his diary entries from mid-January to March, An-sky recounted nearly eight weeks of frenetic traveling. On January 16, he and Ratner reached the city of Radivilov, on the Russian side of the border with Galicia. They spent much of the following week in the vicinity, stalking railroad stations and waiting for their train cars to arrive. On January 23, the men arrived in Brody, their first city in Galicia. After transferring Demidov's shipment onto train cars designed for the narrower gauge of rail lines in Austria, they continued west and reached the provincial capital, Lvov, on January 27. Before sunrise on January 31, a weary An-sky and Ratner straggled into Tarnów. An-sky spent the following two weeks in Tarnów, and on February 14, he returned to the Russian interior to report back to EKOPO committees about his initial findings in Galicia. Over the next two weeks, he made stops in Kiev, Moscow, and Petrograd. By February 26, he was back in Lvov. His last surviving diary entry for winter 1915, dated March 8, found him distributing aid to Jews near Lvov and about to begin a new assignment, traveling around Galicia for the VSG to buy leather for army supplies.

The difficult job of delivering Demidov's supplies to Tarnów occupied most of An-sky's time, but he did not lose sight of his mission as a EKOPO agent. The first thing he did after arriving in any town was to establish contact with an existing Jewish relief committee or community leaders. However, he found few of them. More often, he found lone individuals who had stayed behind, but typically had few or no resources with which to aid the local population. In Tarnów, he found one Dr. Ader, who informed him that of the nearly fifteen thousand Jews

FIGURE 0.4. Boris Efimovich Ratner. *Courtesy of Natasha Ratner.*

estimated to have resided in the city before the war, five thousand were left, among them up to two thousand with no food (January 31, February 1). In Stryi, he met four men whom the Russians had arrested as hostages—business and estate owners—who had formed a "Committee" by giving small amounts of money to people from the windows and doors of their jail cell (March 3).

Because An-sky rarely found relief committees in smaller towns, he set his hopes on organizing aid through the large Jewish community in Lvov, the capital of eastern Galicia, where Jews made up well over a quarter of the city's population (nearly fifty-seven thousand of two hundred thousand total inhabitants). However, there too the Relief Committee had problems. After reaching Lvov on January 27, An-sky sought out two prominent members of the gemina (the Polish equivalent for the Hebrew term *kahal*, or community executive). The first, Herman Diamand, was a socialist politician and publisher, and a former deputy of the Polish Social Democratic Party to the Austrian parliament. Although an avowed assimilationist and Polish nationalist, Diamand was deeply involved in service to the Jewish community. The second, Bernard (Dov) Hausner, a rabbi, Zionist activist, and military chaplain who held a doctorate in philosophy from the German University in Prague, served as the Jewish community's representative to the Russian occupation authorities.[39]

Among the Jews living in Lvov under Russian occupation, nearly four thousand families from the city, as well as another four thousand refugees from the vicinity urgently sought food, clothing, and medicine.[40] Despite the needs of thousands of desperate Jews in Lvov, when An-sky arrived he found the local Relief Committee paralyzed by internal conflicts. The previous fall, David Feinberg, a prominent Jewish lawyer from Kiev, had met with the Russian Governor-General of Galicia, Georgii Bobrinskii, regarding the need to provide philanthropic funds to Jews in Galicia. Although the Army's Chief of Staff Ianushkevich had proposed a prohibition on Jews receiving charitable funds, Bobrinskii, to his credit, managed to oppose it and authorized the formation an official relief committee (called *Va'adat ha-Ezrah* in Hebrew, and *Żydowski Komitet Ratunkowy* in Polish). Lvov's Relief Committee had thus obtained Bobrinskii's official permission to distribute EKOPO funds to the Galician Jews. However, while Hausner was eager to work with EKOPO, Diamand regarded cooperation with Russians, even if they happened to be fellow Jews, as an act of collusion with the enemy. An-sky, under-standably anxious to resolve the dispute between Diamand and Haus-ner so that the local population could begin receiving aid, attempted to mediate between the two men. He was apparently successful in his ef-forts, which are recounted in his diary entries for late February and early March: in the months that followed An-sky's visit to Lvov, the Re-lief Committee, with Diamand as president, Hausner as secretary, and twenty other members, began to use EKOPO funds to distribute food, clothing, and medicine to Jews in the city and surrounding region.[41]

SINISTER OMENS: JEWS, POLES, AND RUTHENIANS (UKRAINIANS) IN RUSSIAN-OCCUPIED GALICIA

As a bilingual aid worker who spoke both Russian and Yiddish, An-sky was able to observe the Russian occupation of Galicia from the vantage points of both the occupying authorities and local Jewish civilians. His diary entries effectively painted a complex picture of the occupation and its highly varied impact on the region's populations of Jews, Poles, and Ruthenians.

An-sky's clothing clearly identified him as a Russian. He wore a uni-form that bore the insignia of a Russian Red Cross worker, with high leather boots and a wool cap. Although he did not intentionally conceal his identity as a Jew, at certain moments he feared being exposed—his given name, the Jewish-sounding Rapoport, was printed in his docu-ments, and on the basis of this alone, police or military authorities could have easily expelled him from Galicia. His appearance as a Russian there-fore gave him cover, especially in his many encounters with Russian officers and troops. From them An-sky heard and recorded remarkable tales of life at the front: stories of Christmas and New Year truces be-tween Russian and German army units (January 20); courageous Rus-sian officers who flung themselves into battle (January 23, February 9); and most frequently, stories of the brutal behavior of Cossacks toward Jews (January 16, February 1, February 28, March 3, March 8, Septem-ber 27, October 8).

An-sky's native knowledge of Yiddish, the vernacular of most Jews in Russia and Galicia, enabled him to communicate with civilians as both an aid worker and a fellow Jew. Wherever his task of moving Demidov's

shipment across Galicia brought him to a shtetl or city with a Jewish community, he sought out businessmen, rabbis, doctors, and in rare cases relief workers to learn about the local population's needs. From the stories he heard and transcribed in his diary, he gradually discovered what the Russian occupation meant for Galicia's Jews: scarcity, hunger, and fear of extreme hostility not only from the Russian military, but also from their Polish and Ruthenian neighbors. Galician Jews were desperate for help and grateful not only for the bit of money, but also the willing ear that An-sky offered them.

Although An-sky was primarily concerned with recording the problems that Jews faced as war victims, his sensibility as an ethnographer and Jewish nationalist expressed itself in a tendency to note signs of resilience, as well as expressions of cultural heritage among them. In Stryi, he talked with a local landowner who was being held hostage by the Russian military. The man told An-sky that he chose not to flee the town after he read a *midrash* (biblical commentary) in which the patriarch Abraham was criticized for leaving the land of Canaan for Egypt when a famine struck (March 3). In Radivilov, An-sky ran into one Gelbort, a man he had met while visiting the town with his Ethnographic Expedition, who told him that during a pogrom in the town, a local man summoned him onto the street to say a blessing over the new moon (January 22).

As An-sky collected stories of military and civilian life, he reflected on how these individual stories and details revealed larger truths about the Russian occupation, and the implications of the Russian authorities' concerted campaign against the Jews. An-sky interpreted the discrete signs he encountered as indications of the Russian authorities' larger and long-term plan: to annex Galicia to the Russian Empire, and as a precondition of doing so, to homogenize the region's multiethnic and multinational character.[42]

Galicia's populations of Poles, Ruthenians, and Jews varied according to its western and eastern regions, which were naturally divided

FIGURE 0.5. An-sky wearing the uniform of a Russian aid worker, 1915. Abram Rekhtman, *Yidishe etnografye un folklor. Zikhroynes vegn der etnografisher ekspeditsye, ongefirt fun Sh. An-ski* (Buenos Aires: YIVO, 1958), 31.

by the San River. The majority of Galician Jews resided on the eastern side, where they made up 13 percent of the population. East Galicia was also home to the majority of the province's Ruthenians, who spoke Ukrainian and belonged to the Greek Catholic Church, or Uniate Church, which incorporated Eastern Orthodox rituals, but recognized the Roman pope as spiritual leader. In contrast, most Galician Poles, who spoke Polish and practiced Roman Catholicism, lived in the West.[43] The Russian government's goal was to integrate the multiethnic, multinational province into Russia's imperial frameworks and to that end, Russian occupation authorities in Galicia sought to politically, economically, and culturally Russify the region. But as An-sky's diary descriptions clearly reveal, Russification politics and practices affected Jews in ways that were far more disastrous than they were for either Poles or Ruthenians.

In September 1914, Bobrinskii enacted an initial set of Russification policies. Amounting to a form of political and cultural occupation, these policies sought to triumphantly promote Russian language and Orthodox faith, while severing the ties of Jews, Poles and Ruthenians to their respective faiths and national cultures. As An-sky traversed Galicia in late January, he observed the impact of five months of Russification policies. On January 25, he heard a story from a Jewish military doctor about a Ruthenian woman who sent her children into hiding after she heard that the Russians planned to forcefully convert them from the Uniate faith to Russian Orthodoxy. An-sky assumed that the woman's story was not an isolated case, but rather an indication of the atmosphere under Russian occupation. Indeed, the Russians' conversion campaign had moved stridently ahead following the arrival in Galicia on December 6, 1914, of the Petrograd Holy Synod's plenipotentiary, Archbishop Evlogii.[44]

An-sky discovered more signs of Russification politics when he reached Lvov on January 27. The city's many names—Lemberg under Austrian rule, Lwów in Polish, and L'viv in Ukrainian—attested to its status as a cultural capital for Poles, Ruthenians, and Jews alike. The city had printing presses and cultural associations for Hebrew, Yiddish, Polish, and Ukrainian and dozens of public and private schools offering instruction in those languages.[45] An-sky noted that Russian occupation authorities had closed down Lvov's national schools (Bobrinskii had done so in mid-September), but reopened them on condition that instruction was to be given in Russian. He discovered Russification policies in effect in smaller cities as well: on February 27, while visiting the town of Zholkva, north of Lvov, An-sky saw that Russian authorities had erased a Polish inscription on a monument to seventeenth-century King Sobiesky, a highly popular monarch during the era of the Polish-Lithuanian Commonwealth.

Yet however much Poles and Ruthenians suffered from attacks on their religions and national cultures, An-sky observed that the impact of Russian occupation practices on Jews had a lethal effect. Russian authorities had embarked on a campaign with a drastic aim to fully deprive Jews of the rights they had enjoyed for almost two generations as citizens of the Habsburg constitutional monarchy, and to reduce, even remove, their presence from the region's economy and civic life.

The concerted anti-Jewish campaign waged by Russian occupation authorities constituted an institutionalized expression of an underlying, almost pathological contempt on the part of Russian military authorities for Jews. Widely disseminated and highly visible military announcements posted throughout Galicia declared Jews to be economic exploiters, spies, and Austrian sympathizers. Claims of alleged "threats" posed by Jews helped to fuel and justify plans voiced by some Russian government authorities to rid the occupied territories of Jews altogether, using whatever means were necessary, whether by "cleansing" them from the region through a series of mass expulsions, or even killing them.[46]

Widely repeated accusations of Jewish espionage also sent the message to rank-and-file troops that Jews were open targets. The stories that An-sky heard repeatedly illustrated how Russians' hostile perceptions of Jews had manifested in violent actions on the ground. He heard of officers who allowed pogroms and gave their troops license to rob Jews or destroy their neighborhoods; Cossacks who forced a son to hang his own father because of a minor offense; and numerous public beatings and humiliations.

Pogroms carried out by passing military units were one of the most common forms of anti-Jewish violence in Galicia. The first anti-Jewish military pogrom in Galicia occurred in Brody in early August 1914, just hours after an advance unit of Cossack troops entered the city. When An-sky reached Brody on January 24, he recorded divergent accounts of it. The version of the story that was most widely circulated, and yet whose authenticity could not be confirmed, was that the Brody pogrom began after a Jewish girl fired a shot from the window of a hotel that killed a Russian officer. Russian troops lynched her on the spot, then killed several Jews and burned the synagogue (in total, nine Jews were killed during the Brody pogrom).[47] An-sky was highly skeptical that a "shooting Jew" had precipitated the violence and was troubled when he heard the same claim surface in accounts of another major pogrom that took place in Lvov on September 27–28, 1914, which left at least a dozen Jews dead.[48]

It was also in Brody and Lvov that An-sky learned about the conspicuous arrests and deportations of Jews. The policies to arrest and deport Jews that were carried out by Russian military and police forces throughout Galicia followed from an order issued by General Ivanov on September 22, 1914, to take Jewish hostages, so as to discourage spying and espionage among the rest of the population.[49] In Lvov, Russian authorities arrested nearly three hundred Jews after the September pogrom, among them Herman Diamand. (When An-sky appeared at Diamand's door on January 27, the latter panicked, assuming An-sky was there to arrest him). And on March 3, in the town of Stryi, An-sky talked for hours with four Jews, local estate owners being held hostage in a room at the local commandant's quarters.

In fact, it was during the second half of January 1915, exactly when An-sky arrived in Galicia, that Russian army commanders began issuing orders to expel Jews, both individuals and in large groups, from different parts of the front zone. At the train station in Radivilov on January 18, An-sky witnessed twenty-four Jews, including a blind, eighty-two-year-old man, being loaded onto unheated train cars in freezing winter temperatures. The Russian Army sent most Jewish expellees from front zones in Galicia east to the Kiev, Chernigov, and Poltava provinces in the Russian interior.

As an ethnographer, An-sky was keenly aware of the destructive impact of military violence not only on Jews as people, but also on their culture. Wherever soldiers looted and burned Jewish quarters, they

FIGURE 0.6. Children in Sochachew, Poland, stand near Torah scrolls that were desecrated by the Russian Army during World War I. *Courtesy of the* YIVO *Institute for Jewish Research, New York.*

also destroyed centuries-old synagogues, Torah scrolls, sacred ritual objects, books, and libraries. In the small town of Tuchów, he listened to a tearful woman recount how she had seen Russian troops pillage hidden Torah scrolls from the synagogue and trample them on horseback in the street (February 8). The day before, also in Tuchów, An-sky entered a wrecked synagogue and later recorded what is among the most searing accounts in his diary:

> The synagogue is big and new; it was built eleven years ago. It wasn't burned, but the windows are broken, the doors are wide open, and inside all that remains is an ark with gilding. Everything else was decimated. There is no pulpit, no platform, no benches, no lights, no scrolls—nothing. The walls are bare. There are scraps of religious books and chandelier fragments lying scattered about on the floor mixed up with straw. The corners of the room and adjoining chapels were fouled, not by horses, but by people. They turned a temple into a latrine.

In addition to the destructive impact of Russian occupation policies on Jewish cultural life and spaces, such policies also imposed extreme economic hardships on Jews. As part of the effort to minimize the place of Jews in the local economy, Russian military authorities seized land-holdings, ordered that the military cease all business relations with Jewish suppliers, and fired Jews employed in civil service jobs.[50] The latter fate befell a Hasidic man whom An-sky saw in a Brody synagogue on January 24. As another congregant at the synagogue explained to him, "With long *peyes*, he used to deliver letters, was considered a gov-ernment worker, earned a living. And now he's dying of hunger." As a result of the poverty, scarcity of goods, hunger, diseases, and destruction caused by bombings and fires, the mortality rate of Jews in the Lvov region spiked during the winter and spring of 1915.[51]

An-sky's diary entries also recounted incidents that revealed Poles' and Ruthenians' reactions to the treatment of Jews under Russian oc-cupation. Tensions between Jews, Poles, and Ruthenians had grown in the years before the war, especially after 1907, when elections were held following the Austro-Hungarian enactment of suffrage reform. The 1907 elections marked the first time that Jews had voted deci-sively as a bloc for their own national interests, rather than for the Pol-ish national cause, which they had previously supported. This deci-sive shift of political loyalties among Jews engendered open hostility from Poles.[52] The eminent scholar of Jewish history, Salo Baron, who grew up in Tarnów, in western Galicia, and fled west to Cracow just before the Russians arrived in the fall of 1914, described himself as having been a strong supporter of Polish nationalism in his youth. Yet after 1907, he recalled, he began to question his loyalties, as the "in-bred antisemitism of the Christian population came pronouncedly to the fore."[53]

In East Galicia as well, both Poles and Ruthenians (who formed 22 and 65 percent of the population, respectively), harbored bitter feelings for Jews, whom they identified as oppressive owners and overseers of the region's oil fields and landed estates.[54] Even though there were Jews who worked in the oil fields as unskilled laborers, Ruthenian peasants and workers nevertheless associated Jews with the much-loathed overseers and foremen. And in all of Galicia, only a few hundred Jewish families owned estates (561 of the region's 2,550 estates, and among the smallest ones at that). The Polish landowning class, for their part, resented the

Jews' ownership of estates that had previously belonged to Poles and refused to accept them as equals.[55]

The stories that An-sky heard throughout Galicia revealed that the Russian forces were aware of the Poles' and Ruthenians' preexisting hostility toward Jews and were keen to exploit it for their own purposes. He heard of Russian commanders who tried to win the Galician peasants' loyalty with gestures indicating how Jewish landowners would be treated in Russia—a finger drawn across the neck (January 25); Cossacks who ordered Jews on an estate to kiss the exposed backsides of Ruthenian peasants (February 1); and soldiers who rewarded local peasants for uncovering hidden Jewish property with some of the spoils (March 3).

The most visible and worrisome sign of the growing distance between Jews and their neighbors, however, were religious icons that Poles and Ruthenians placed in the doors and windows of their homes to identify them, in the event of a pogrom, as Christians and not Jews. These icons, which he described after seeing them in Stryi on March 3, had been "placed in the windows of all the Christian houses, as if a pogrom is expected at any minute." He had also seen icons earlier in Lvov, Brody, and Rzeszów—"throughout all of Galicia," as he wrote, a "sinister omen" (January 23)—symbols that expressed the neighbors' acknowledgment and perhaps even approval that the Jews had become open targets under Russian occupation.

AN-SKY IN PETROGRAD

The surviving text of An-sky's diary for winter 1915 ceases on March 8 in the small town of Lubaczów, fifty miles northwest of Lvov. The second existing fragment of his diary resumes on September 9, 1915, in Petrograd. During the six months from March to September 1915, Russia's position in the war and the fate of Jews in military-occupied zones both took a radical turn for the worse. German forces drove the Russians back hundreds of miles along the Northwest Front, and by the end of summer, they were in control of a vast part of western Russia, including the cities of Warsaw, Vilna, and Brest-Litovsk. As Russian army units retreated to the east, they systematically sought to remove the so-called unreliable Jewish populations from various regions by deporting entire communities, including nearly the whole population of Jews residing in Kurland and Kovno provinces.[56]

In May 1915, Austro-Hungarian forces inflicted another series of shattering defeats on the Russian Army's Southwest Front. By the end of the summer, the Austrians had retaken nearly all of Galicia and Bukovina. Still doing aid work for EKOPO in Galicia at the time, An-sky was swept up in the massive Russian retreat. He moved east in a stream of demoralized troops and expelled civilians, including nearly fifty thousand Jews deported by the Russian Army.[57] To accommodate the large and growing numbers of expellees, most of whom were deported to the easternmost parts of the Pale of Settlement, the tsar's Council of Ministers voted in August 1915 to provisionally expand the borders of the Pale, allowing Jews to settle in the Russian interior, with the exception of Moscow, Petrograd, and Cossack territories.[58]

Over the summer of 1915 An-sky found his way back to Petrograd. He returned to a city that was reeling from workers' strikes, and food and firewood shortages. He observed public discontent with the government become increasingly visible on the streets. Drained from nearly eight months of constant travel across the front zone, he set up a makeshift home inside the Jewish Historical-Ethnographic Society's main building, in the city's historic center on Vasilievsky Island.[59] His residence in Petrograd was tenuous, however, for although the Pale had been effectively abolished in August, the capital city remained off limits to Jews unless they possessed an official residence permit, which An-sky did not. Throughout his diary entries for this period one finds descriptions of his frustrated efforts to secure a permit from the Minister of the Interior, N. B. Shcherbatov, and his various appeals for the help from prominent Jewish representatives such as M. A. Varshavskii and Sliozberg, influential friends such as Naidich, and officials inside the halls of the Department of Public Affairs.

An-sky's diary entries for September and October, which he did not incorporate into *The Destruction of Galicia*, portray a world apart from the ruined towns and desperate people he had met in occupied Galicia. These passages were written in terse, sometimes cryptic fragments, with a tone that shifted between that of a passionate enthusiast and harsh critic. An-sky focused on descriptions of his political and cultural work in Petrograd and Moscow, as well as observations of what appeared to be imminent signs of major political changes, if not the revolution he hoped would come.

In September and October, An-sky also threw himself into efforts to stage his Russian-language play, *The Dybbuk*, a tragic love story about spirit possession and Hasidic Jews set in a shtetl that resembled the types he had visited during his ethnographic expedition.[60] These diary entries provide a fascinating chronicle of the play's history and development. An-sky recounted his woefully unsuccessful attempts to have the original Russian version of his play performed on the Russian stage. He met with Russian theater directors in Petrograd and Moscow, revised the play according to their instructions, read the play for groups of his Jewish friends, and discussed it with Russian writers such as the Silver Age poet F. K. Sologub. Ultimately he despaired in his hopes to stage it in Russia. The diary thus reveals the inauspicious origins of a play that later became known as An-sky's masterpiece in its Hebrew and Yiddish versions, and one of the most famous works of Jewish theater in the world.

An-sky's diary for the fall of 1915 also described his newfound embrace of militant Zionism, "the idea," as he wrote on September 27, "that Jews can go out with weapons in their hands in defense of their national rights." He gave a number of speeches in Petrograd in support of the Zionist Vladimir Jabotinsky's Jewish Legion, a fighting unit that served with the British Army with the aim of liberating Palestine from Ottoman authority. An-sky wrote of the tremendous, scathing opposition that the idea of the legion encountered from most Russian Zionists, who conformed with the official policy of the World Zionist Organization to avoid ties to Allied powers so long as Palestine remained under Ottoman control.[61] An-sky also told of his meetings in Petrograd with the socialist, philosemitic writer Maksim Gorky (which he held at Jabotinsky's request) to enlist the latter's support on behalf of the legion.

Despite the geographical and psychological distance that separated home front and war zone, the war remained a constant presence in An-sky's writings and interactions. His memories of Galicia were still fresh, and like a red thread, the attempt to defend and rescue Jewish war victims ran

throughout his accounts of his political and cultural work in the fall of
1915. He characterized Petrograd's activists as being aloof from the crisis facing the Jewish masses and urged them to travel to the war zone, as
he had done, "to see what is happening with their own eyes" (October 8).
Not surprisingly, he managed to provoke debates at meetings of EKOPO,
the Jewish Historical-Ethnographic Society, and the Jewish Artist's
Society. The suffering Jews of Galicia haunted his disparate efforts:
strengthening Jewish cultural nationalism in Russia, supporting Jewish
fighters who could liberate a homeland for diaspora Jewry, and defend-
ing the image of Jews before Russian public opinion.

A RUSSIAN AND JEWISH WAR DIARY

It is highly likely that An-sky used Yiddish in his daily interactions
with Jewish civilians in war zones throughout Galicia and Russia. Yet he
chose to write his war diary in Russian, the language he most frequently
used in his own circles, and the one in which he wrote most of his literary work. But by 1916, An-sky had made a decision to translate the diary
from Russian into Yiddish and Hebrew. An-sky's choice to present the
diary in all three languages prompts the question of how to identify his
Russian-language diary in cultural and literary terms. An-sky's motives
and intentions as a diarist are important to reflect upon in this regard.

An-sky's choice to write in multiple languages reflected his wish to
convey his knowledge and experiences of the war to diverse audiences of
readers. As we noted earlier, his larger aim was to write a testimony and
provide a historical record of the war for future generations, including
Jews who would ostensibly read his account in Yiddish or Hebrew. However, at the time of the war itself, his immediate goal was to relate information about Russia's anti-Jewish campaign in Galicia to persons of influence in Russian society. In his diary, he recounted meetings in the winter
and fall of 1915 in which he discussed the persecution of Galician Jewry
with EKOPO committees and the director, Sliozberg (September 10); Russian politicians and literary figures, including the Kadet Party leader P. N.
Miliukov (February 21), and the poet Sologub (February 19, October 1);
and editors of Russian liberal newspapers (January 12).

For An-sky, keeping his diary in Russian thus served a practical
purpose. His diary functioned in effect like a field reporter's notebook,

where he recorded information such as estimates of local populations of Jews and non-Jews; events that followed the Russian occupation; and lists of the locals' most pressing material needs, including food, money, medicine, and shelter. An-sky used this information in his reports to EKOPO committees in Petrograd, Moscow, and Kiev during the weeks of January 6 to 14, and again from February 17 to 25. EKOPO's leaders, in turn, relied on factual evidence relayed by An-sky and other relief workers in their own reports to the Russian government, and international philanthropic organizations such as the Joint Distribution Committee, which held EKOPO accountable for millions of rubles.[62]

The private nature of An-sky's diary also allowed him to record information that wartime military censors would not have allowed in print and was therefore all the more important to convey verbally to groups such as EKOPO. A most difficult topic that An-sky discussed in several places throughout the diary was the rape of women, both Jews and non-Jews, in Galicia. When he arrived in Lvov, for example, he learned from Hausner that Russian troops had raped forty girls in Buczacz (January 28); from a Jewish military doctor in Galicia named Gil'man, he learned that Cossacks had attempted to rape a fifty-eight-year-old woman in the small town of Cieszanów, as well as two young girls in Głogów, who were killed along with their parents when the latter stepped in to defend them (February 1). Even after the war, rape remained a difficult subject to broach in print, including publications intended for Jewish audiences. In 1918, Dubnov edited and published a compilation of documents about anti-Jewish atrocities, known as the "Black Book of Russian Jewry." Among the atrocities described there he included accounts of rape, along with the names of women and locations where they had occurred. Dubnov later received a letter from a reader in Moscow who condemned him for having put the women's "woes on display" by publishing their names.[63] This reaction to the "Black Book" underscores the importance of An-sky's decision to write about rape in his diary, as it produced written evidence, or a historical record, of the distinct ways in which Jewish women had suffered during the war—the knowledge of which was stifled after the war.

An-sky also sought to publish his war writings in multiple languages because he believed that Hebrew, Yiddish, *and* Russian were all languages that could serve as mediums for Jewish cultural expression.[64]

He undertook efforts to publish his war writings in those three languages before the war had even ended. By 1916, he had completed an eight-page summary of his diaries from 1914 to 1915 in Russian.[65] In mid-1917, he sold the rights to a Hebrew edition of his writings about Galicia to Stybel Press in Moscow (it was not published until 1929). By April 1918, he had completed the first volume of his war memoir in Yiddish.[66]

After settling in Vilna in September 1918, An-sky devoted the following year and a half to writing the Yiddish version of his war story. That he chose to write his memoir in Yiddish while living in postwar Vilna was hardly surprising. The city became a hub for numerous Russian-speaking Jewish intellectuals who began to use Yiddish specifically as a language for supporting the cause of Jewish cultural nationalism. In 1919, Abraham Cahan, the Vilna-born writer who emigrated to the United States and became editor of New York's largest Yiddish daily, *Forverts*, traveled to his native city. He might easily have been speaking of An-sky when he wrote, "Jewish intellectuals who for thirty or forty years have only spoken Russian are now speaking Yiddish."[67] Like An-sky, other Russified Jewish intellectuals in Vilna, including his friend (and for a time personal physician) Jacob Wygodski, chose to write their war memoirs not in Russian, but in Yiddish.[68] And An-sky must have surely known that his close friend Dr. Tsemakh Shabad (mentioned in his diary on January 31, after the two crossed paths in Tarnów) was compiling an anthology of documents about Jewish life in German-occupied Vilna for publication in Yiddish.[69]

As An-sky worked on *The Destruction of Galicia* in Vilna, he continued to engage in aid work and cultural work as he had during the war. In 1919, he established a local EKOPO division in the city, and that same year, he founded a new Jewish Historical-Ethnographic Society. Modeled after its predecessor in Petrograd, this organization later inspired the formation, in Vilna in 1925, of the Yiddish Scientific Institute (*Yidisher Visnshaftlekher Institut*, or YIVO), which became the world's foremost organization dedicated to the study, preservation, and teaching of Yiddish language and East European Jewish history.[70]

After completing work on *The Destruction of Galicia*, An-sky expressed his hope that his memoir's portrayal of Jewish life in war-torn Eastern Europe would remain compelling to current and future generations of readers, both in Europe and in the new world. While convalescing in Warsaw in October 1920, he wrote to his lifelong friend Chaim Zhitlowsky about his memoir, explaining why he thought the Yiddish press in New York might want to publish it. He referred to the recent appearance in Warsaw of Polish-born Jews who had moved to America, but who had returned to their native city as tourists. They had brought cameras to take films of Polish Jewry to show their friends and family in America. As An-sky watched them filming their old homes, he thought of his own effort to describe how East European Jews had lived during the war: "My book is also a kind of *moving pictures*, with descriptions of 200 cities and shtetls in Poland, Galicia, and Bukovina, saying what happened there and mentioning hundreds of local Jews."[71]

The cultural and historical significance that *The Destruction of Galicia* would hold for later generations was something he could have scarcely imagined at the time. Less than two decades passed between his death in 1920 and the beginning of the next world war. An-sky could not have foreseen that war, or the catastrophic impact it would have on the Jews of Eastern Europe. Yet by the start of the Second World War, his descriptions of Russian-occupied Galicia served as touchstones for contemporary events. In late 1939, the American Jewish historian Abraham Duker wrote an essay in which he compared the brutalities that the German Army unleashed in western Poland after September 1939 to An-sky's descriptions of Russian Army atrocities in Galicia in 1915.[72] And in March 1943, the extraordinarily prolific diarist in the Vilna ghetto Herman Kruk recalled the violence, hunger, forced labor, and despair that he had read about "years ago" in An-sky's memoir. Even with An-sky's tales of horror as a point of reference, Kruk could not grasp the depths of his own generation's suffering: "If it was unbearable there," he wrote, "what is our life?"[73]

After the Holocaust, excerpts from *The Destruction of Galicia* were printed in a new genre of Jewish literature known as memorial books—anthologies published in Yiddish or Hebrew to commemorate the history of individual East European Jewish communities whose residents, often the compilers' own family members, became martyrs during the war. More than 1,400 memorial books have been published in Israel and North America since the 1950s. An-sky's wartime writings about Galicia's

cities and small towns appeared in some of them, including those for
Zholkva and Rzeszow, both towns that he visited and described, first in
his diary from 1915, and later again in *The Destruction of Galicia*.[74] With
this publication, An-sky's war diary can finally take its place alongside
The Destruction of Galicia as a testimony to the vanished world of East
European Jewry. These surviving fragments of war and revolution re-
store glimpses of an increasingly distant, yet transformative chapter of
world history.

S. An-sky's

1915 *Diary*

Winter 1915
Galicia

JANUARY 1, ROVNO[1]

The new year was born in profound melancholy. Neither desires nor hopes, as though you were standing before a corpse. I spent the day in a miserable state. At night I went to the "Yiddish Theater." They were offering a senseless operetta, *Khontse in America*. The most untalented of the untalented performed. But the theater was packed and the audience was in ecstasy.

Met a friendly military doctor, Kon, whose wife is working as a nurse in the field hospital. They invited me to visit the hospital tomorrow and see how it was set up.

JANUARY 2

I didn't feel well. At night I went to the hospital. A huge hospital with many beds, superbly equipped. Clean, spacious. There are paintings of battle scenes plastered across all of the walls. A number of wounded Austrians are lying on beds mixed in among the Russians.

"But how did you get along with the Austrians, don't you quarrel?" I asked a wounded Russian.

"Why should we quarrel? All of us are cursed," he replied with profound sorrow.

I went to the dressing station. They were dressing wounds on 218 Austrians who had just arrived. The wounds are something terrible. The entry wound is small; the exit wound is huge. These are our hollow-point bullets. Upon striking a target, they begin to spin in all directions.

They showed me a man who had been stabbed by a bayonet eleven times. He is recovering.

There was an Austrian lying on the dressing table whose leg had been amputated at the knee. The leg was exposed in preparation for bandaging. The bone was sticking out, with a chunk of nervously twitching red meat. Nothing so terrible about it. Meat. But then, a hand, from which all the skin between the fingers and wrist had been ripped away, made an impression on me? That isn't a piece of protruding flesh, but a wound surrounded by the body's healthy parts.

JANUARY 3

I visited the hospital again. Such suffering! The dressing of wounds alone elicits so much agony. Here, for example, is someone who was "lightly wounded": the bullet tore through the flesh of his leg, scrotum, and flesh of the other leg. Gauze must be drawn through the whole wound.

I walked among the beds. There was a wounded Austrian lying on a bed. He was no older than a boy, with a red button-shaped nose and swollen eyes. He has a broken leg and a gunshot wound in the chest. And apart from that he has a broken jaw and his lower teeth were knocked out. He talks in a feverish manner and his speech is not altogether intelligible. He addresses the nurse like an offended child, complains. The bed is too hard; it chafes his sides. And the food.... They are supposed to serve him different food, it seems.

"Yes, yes," the nurse consoles him, "you'll get milk, kasha."

"I'm not allowed to eat the meat that you give all of them," the wounded boy goes on, ignoring her. "The doctor said. But I am allowed to eat cutlets. And they should be made with onion—with onion! *Viel Zwiebel, viel Zwiebel.*[2] Doctor's orders ..."

A few hours later his wounds were dressed, and it seems that when the nurses bandaged his leg five days ago they put in a splint that was too long, and it left a palm-sized sore on his side and nearly punctured his stomach. And here with such injuries, with a splint eating away at a festering wound, he thinks about *viel Zwiebel*—even alleges that the doctor prescribed them. He must have associated the relief of his misery with this favorite food.

Had dinner with Dr. Kon. His wife told me that Andre, a local marshal of the nobility, is organizing a medical transport to Galicia and would probably agree to take me with him. Mrs. Kon promised to find out about it tomorrow and put in a word on my behalf.

I came back to the hotel at about eight o'clock and found a telegram from Naidich[3] in Moscow: "Come to Moscow. Demidov's division departs for Kiev and beyond on January 7. There is a spot for someone."

Can it be that my affairs are finally falling into place and my ordeals will come to an end?

I left for Moscow at eleven o'clock at night. An announcement was hanging in the train station: "Reward for capture of spies: 10 to 150 rubles, and gratitude from His Majesty and country."

JANUARY 4

There was a lieutenant riding in the train with me who was just returning from a post at the Prussian Front.[4] He was quiet, modest, as are most of the heroes who have been in combat. He recounted many interesting things.

The men grew so accustomed to cannon fire that when it was quiet they felt frightened and anxious. They got to know the places where the bombs landed because the other side always fired at specific spots. Bombs that fell at close range gave off gasses that caused terrible vomiting in some of the men. The most terrible thing, though, is that the wounded must remain in the trenches the whole day; they can only be moved at night, and sometimes not even then.

"Before their new year we wrote greeting cards on scraps of paper, freed up a shrapnel shell, stuffed it with the papers, and shot it over.[5] The shell didn't explode, but it seems they found the cards. But then we were angry with them because on Christmas they shot at us like the damned, so at midnight of the new year we started firing at them with all of our guns.

"Our artillery works well, but their side is better equipped. They'll go up in an airplane, find our battery and shoot a rocket. With that rocket they can precisely pinpoint the location of our battery from a distance, within two degrees. For some reason our side doesn't do this.

"Theft and looting are scourges of war. When the soldiers enter a city or town they start to rob the locals. I know of one case in Galicia: an officer entered a house and saw the soldiers looting. They took off running. He ordered them to stop. They disobeyed. He shot and killed two of them. The other three stopped. He ordered that one hundred lashes be given to each of them and sent them to the trenches. The medical orderlies are constantly being searched, but it doesn't help. Sometimes they even kill our officers and rob them.

"Some of the nurses work selflessly, of course. But most of the ones in the rear behave indecently; they sleep with doctors, wreak debauchery, depravity. They aren't called sisters of mercy, but rather 'whores of mercy.'"

The lieutenant also recited the legend about the Grand Duke[6] and Rennenkampf,[7] how the latter seemingly wounded the former.

It seems the Grand Duke summoned his quartermasters, came to them darker than a storm cloud, and said, "If you keep secrets, I will hang you."

One encounters strange sights. A soldier comes to ask for a stretcher so he can be evacuated on it. He was shot in the head. Another in the trenches asks for permission to go to the dressing clinic. "Where were you wounded?" "In the head," he replies, and points to his crown. "From where did the bullet emerge?" "From the buttocks, your Excellency."

JANUARY 5, MOSCOW

Naidich told me how simply my trip had been arranged. Igor Platonovich Demidov,[8] a deputy to the State Duma, is stationed with a division in Galicia, in Tarnów. If I had been in Moscow a few days earlier I could have left with him. Now Igor Platonovich's brother, Lev Platonovich,[9] who directs the Moscow division, is sending several train cars with hospital supplies and linens to the Tarnów division. And here they are assigning me to be the plenipotentiary who is responsible for delivering these train cars. Another plenipotentiary, an assistant barrister named B. E. Ratner[10] will travel with me, along with an *artel*[11] worker, who will look after the cars.

I went to see L. P. Demidov; he makes a wonderful impression, as a man of profound, sensitive, and cultured ideals, and is fanatically devoted to the cause. We arranged all of the details. I will of course pay my own way, but the committee[12] will supply my train fare. The train cars depart on the 9th, not the 7th, so I'll have time for a trip to Petrograd.

I telephoned Nikolai Aleksandrovich Popov.[13] He promised to connect me with Vladimir Ivanovich Nemirovich-Danchenko[14] in a few days, and arrange for me to read him the play.[15]

JANUARY 6, PETROGRAD

I gave a report about what I saw and heard in Poland. In light of the short notice there wasn't time to assemble a significant number of people. Bramson,[16] Braudo,[17] Bikerman,[18] Brusilovskii, Levin, Pozner,[19] and a few others were there. It seems the report made a very strong impression, especially the facts. These were my conclusions: 1) To set up as few soup kitchens as possible, and instead give more aid to each individual refugee, to help him get back on his feet; 2) To appoint two or three people in Warsaw who can manage activities there; 3) To urgently organize a large (Russian-language) newspaper in Warsaw.

S. V. Pozner told me what has been happening lately in Petrograd. The most interesting and important thing is the creation by the finest representatives of Russian literature of a league to fight for Jewish emancipation.[20] Gorky,[21] Andreev,[22] and Sologub[23] are its leaders and have passionately taken up the cause.

The conference of December 19 resulted merely in a declaration. The people who gathered at the conference were mostly anemic and didn't introduce any initiatives.

At the editorial office of *The Day*,[24] I found out that all of my articles were received, and that the censor crossed all of them out, which is why they weren't printed.

I obtained copies for the museum[25] of Austrian propaganda for Jews that was thrown from planes and written in Yiddish and Hebrew.

JANUARY 8

I spent yesterday and today in Petrograd; saw Sliozberg,[26] Vinaver,[27] and others. Everyone seems to believe that agitation against Jews in Poland is quieting down. A relative of Vinaver's even reasoned that in Warsaw the Poles' attitudes have greatly changed. But all of this strikes me as complacency.

JANUARY 9, MOSCOW

The train cars depart on the 11th.

Naidich told me a curious thing.

The Ministry of Foreign Affairs summoned Rozov[28] as a representative of Zionism. Since Rozov wasn't in Petrograd at the time, they invited Idelson.[29] In Turkey, demands were issued that Russian Jews must adopt Turkish citizenship or else face expulsion.[30] Because the Russian government doesn't wish to lose the element in Palestine that has ties to Russia, the ministry asked Idelson to inform the colonists in a telegram that he advises them to become Turkish subjects. If they do so, the ministry promises to reinstate them after the war as subjects who adopted foreign residency under duress. Idelson replied that such a telegram wouldn't get through to the colonists there; the ministry then requested only that he compose and relay the telegram to the ministry, and it would attempt to deliver it on its own.

JANUARY 10

I reported at the Relief Society[31] here too about the situation in Poland, as well as my upcoming trip. The question of whether to supply me with funds for hunger relief in Galicia was raised. But not all of the committee's members were present and the question was deferred until the 12th.

JANUARY 12

Yesterday and today I met with Popov, who brought me to see an actor at the Moscow Art Theater, Georgii Sergeevich Burdzhalov.[32] Popov had promised to connect me with Nemirovich-Danchenko, but nothing came of it, as Nemirovich is tough to catch.

I met with the journalist Ivan Vasilievich Johnson,[33] whose acquaintance I made last fall at Popov's house. He promised he would try to get Nemirovich-Danchenko to read the play after my departure.

≈

Ordynskii[34] returned from Tarnów. Ratner and I went to see him. He described his impressions. He witnessed the explosion of a forty-two–centimeter shell.[35] His impressions were extremely depressing and difficult. He won't travel there again under any circumstances.

In addition to Ordynskii's correspondence, Ganeizer's[36] articles have been printed in *Russian News*.[37] This means that my agreements fell through. It's true that Engel and Ordynskii are proposing that I write, but somehow I'm not inspired.

I tried to enter into an agreement through Johnson with *Russia's Morning*[38] and *Voice of Moscow*,[39] which have both altered their features, but nothing came of it.

Yesterday the train cars were sent to Gomel and Sarna. I'm taking the express train to Kiev today.

JANUARY 13

The trip has been dull. There are three other young people traveling with me, plenipotentiaries for the Union of Towns[40] who are bringing four train cars to the Carpathians. The cars will travel with ours and under our name until we reach Lvov. It seems they're young people, students, but they show little interest. They play cards the whole time.

I thought of dropping in to see my cousin in Seredina Buda[41] but didn't have time. At the railroad station, I ran into Dr. Lazarev, an acquaintance of mine. He had been on leave in Buda and saw my family. Now he's headed for the front. He mentioned some things about the poor treatment of Jews.

JANUARY 14, KIEV

As always, I was greeted with a warm, caring welcome in Kiev. Mazor,[42] Makhover[43] and Syrkin[44] received me like family. Several people gathered soon after to whom I gave a report. They listened with great interest. Bykhovskii[45] kept trying to prove that Jews themselves are to blame for many things, that they don't behave tactfully. But what he wanted wasn't clear. While Gepner[46] was parting with me after the conclusion of the report, he said he hoped I would return from Galicia with happier impressions.

"There is little hope of that," I replied, "although perhaps I could bring some happiness to the Galician Jews."

He understood me, then took out and handed me 500 rubles.

"Nobody can put this money to better use than you," he said.

It turns out that the campaign I started in Kiev to collect clothing last October was a huge success. The drive produced brilliant results. There are now 750 pood[47] of clothing. Much of it was sent away. What is most important above all, though, is that a society to provide aid to war victims throughout all of Russia was established in connection with this clothing drive.

JANUARY 14

I went to see the baron.[48] He has hardly changed. He's in exactly the same form as he was three months ago: cheerful, energetic, trim. Still the same sweet, charming man, with a big heart. I had breakfast with him, and over breakfast I spoke about my impressions and observations. I also talked about my imminent trip to Galicia.

Two hours after I left, the baron's secretary brought me 3,000 rubles for Galicia.

≈

Ratner arrived after having spent an extra day in Moscow. We decided to stay in Kiev until tomorrow. It's all the same, since the train won't reach Radivilov before we do.

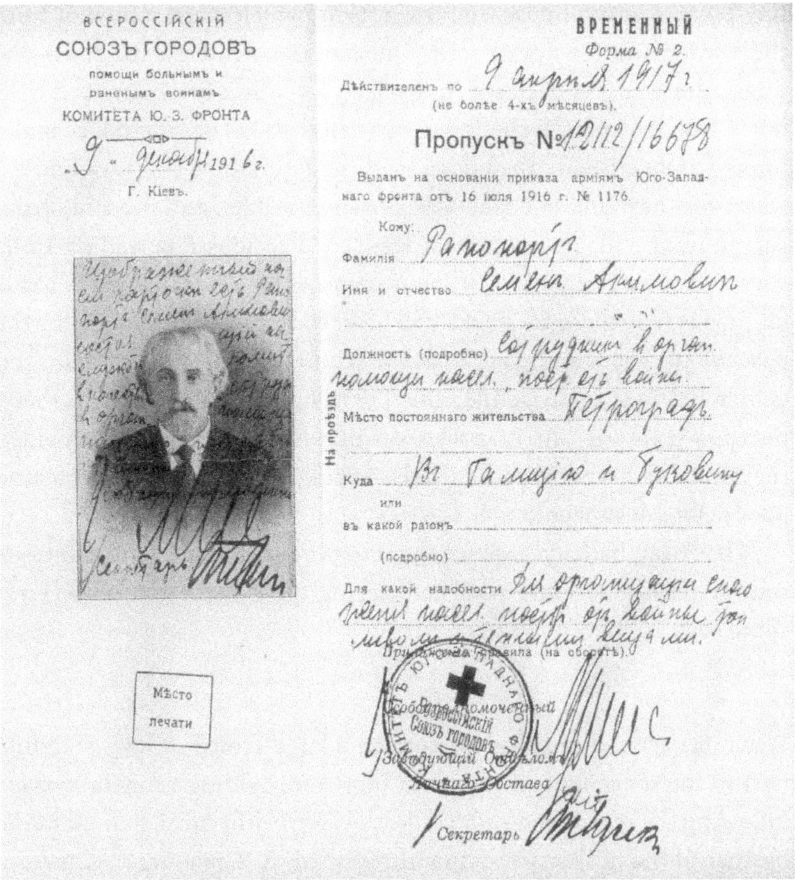

FIGURE 1.1. Document granting An-sky permission to travel to Galicia and Bukovina as an aid worker for the All-Russian Union of Towns during the war. *Gezamelte shriftn in fuftsen bender,* 15 vols. (Vilna: Farlag "An-sky," 1920–1925), 4: n.p. (after 119).

JANUARY 15

We left in the evening.

JANUARY 16, RADIVILOV[49]

A large border shtetl. At first glance it appears to be full of life. There is a crowd of soldiers in the market, brisk bargaining. However, complete ruin is concealed behind this exterior. Apart from the destruction of the town's custom-house, the town itself, which made its living from the border, was also destroyed. The Austrians entered the town one week after war was declared, but stayed for only a few hours and then left. Cossacks entered the town right after they left, and bacchanalia immediately ensued. They destroyed the best stores and warehouses; whatever they couldn't take was smashed to bits, and peasants from surrounding villages took what was left. Precious few trading stalls survived the destruction, which continued for several days. What is curious is that these Cossacks had been stationed in Radivilov for the past twelve years and were familiar with everyone. Several hundred people hid in the synagogue. The Cossacks wanted to break in there, but apparently one Christian who was guarding them came out, shielded the door with his body, and started to rebuke the Cossacks for attacking poor defenseless people.

It has been half a year since then, but life still hasn't returned to its routine. Many of those who fled during the destruction haven't yet come back.

≈

When we arrived in town we noticed a large crowd of Jews standing next to the synagogue. It turns out they were holding a funeral service following the recent and sudden death of a wealthy local, Samuil Mess, brother of the millionaire-philanthropist M. A. Ginzburg.[50] Ginzburg did a lot for his native shtetl—he built an extravagant hospital, opened schools, constructed synagogues, founded various charities. In addition he spent 30,000 to 40,000 rubles on the shtetl every year. He managed all of these charitable activities through his brother.

I met this Mess about two years ago while visiting Radivilov. He was short, not very intelligent, and a person of little culture. However, it was clear he had a kind heart and fit the role of a patron. When the war began, he went to Petrograd and lived with his brother. He left for Galicia a week ago to distribute money to Jews who lost everything, but two days later he suddenly died in one shtetl. His body was brought here and will be buried today.

His death plunged the whole town into profound despair. People are talking about it with tears in their eyes, like a calamity that is more terrible than the war. The shtetl has been deprived of its defender, father, breadwinner.

≈

The train cars haven't gotten here yet and it is unclear when they'll arrive. There is a backup along the Zdolbunov-Radivilov line (single track). Echelon after echelon of the Finland Corps speedily passes by, but still moves more slowly than it should. All kinds of other cargo have been delayed. It's certain that our train cars have gotten stuck somewhere. The station sentry said, "God willing, they should arrive by the 20th."

JANUARY 17

The train cars aren't here. We go to the station several times a day to inquire. The sentry sent telegrams along the whole line with inquiries, but we can expect a reply only tomorrow.

We landed in a filthy hotel, a den. It's dirty, bleak. Our companions, the Union of Towns plenipotentiaries, are some kind of fools. One is a typical Khlestakov;[51] he lies, brags, acts like a commander, shouts, gives orders. He is the complete embodiment of stupidity. The theme of his conversations: girls—until I put him in his place. The second one is fairly intelligent, neither a fool nor a stupid man, but there is something positively idiotic about him. He rolls his eyes in some sort of strange way. When faced with the simplest situation, in which one needs to think, make a decision, and express an opinion, he becomes confused, and pitifully, helplessly gazes at those around him in a plea for help. He has some kind of passion for filth. He enjoys digging at his foot fungus in front of everyone, takes pleasure in rubbing his boots with his hand, and not only his boots but all of us too. He rants and raves behind Nikolai (Kirikov's) back, but is fearful, submissive in his presence. The third boy, with ruddy cheeks, writes dozens of letters and makes copies of them. Were it not for Ratner (a very smart and decent person, although like some other Marxists a bit harsh and rigid), I might lose my mind from boredom.

Echelon after echelon is passing through the train station. Soldiers who are headed for the front encounter the returning wounded and greedily question them. One little soldier's phrase, a question that was uttered with great anguish, pointedly imprinted itself: "Will 'she' make peace soon?" "She" is the war.[52]

In front of the station in a large square there is a mass of people bargaining for bread, sausage, tea, and other cheap foods. Soldiers are buying things, drinking, eating. And the square resembles a military headquarters. Toward nightfall Austrian prisoners appeared on the square in their thin blue-gray coats, boots, and peaked caps. The clothing is totally unsuitable for the winter. There is frost. Even without the clothes they are pitiable, cowed, even doubled over, hiding their hands close to their chests. It is just a pity.

Trains carrying the wounded pass by one after another. I spent some time in one of them. It was remarkably well equipped.

Red Cross train no. 196 arrived from Kiev, on its way to Brody to pick up the wounded. We met the staff. A female doctor, nurses. They are strikingly sweet, hardworking, dedicated people. One nurse, E. K. Karas, a Polish woman, made an especially nice, charming impression. They invited us to go with them to Brody. Ratner and I went.

On the train there was a dignified old man, a depressed and troubled peasant. I questioned him. It seems he traveled here from Ufa province with a train car full of gifts worth 3,000 rubles from two parishes and a monastery. And for the past two weeks now his train car has been stuck without moving. What place is there for gifts when troops and weapons have to be transported? He understands this, but is thoroughly exhausted and confused. How he had longed for this! Each peasant kopek that was sacrificed is a feat. And he had expected that this widow's mite would be greeted with joy, with rapture. And suddenly, he and his gifts are unnecessary; he must kneel down, pray, wait for a few weeks, and sustain himself. And bitter pain is growing in his soul.

Brody—a decent city.[53] The whole street that leads from the railroad station is in shambles on both sides; chimneys protrude, collapsed roofs are on the ground. The war came through here nearly five months ago with all of her horrors, and the traces are still gaping wounds.

The little town appears full of life outside. But throngs of poor children run you over at every turn. I gave several of them each one coin, was about to give one to another, and suddenly one of the first I'd given to screams at me with horror in his eyes: "Don't give him anything—he's a Jew!"

I stopped by the Bristol Hotel to see Feigenbaum. I was told he is living with Dr. Kalakh in the building next door. The doctor's wife, a dignified old woman, greeted me at the door. At first she was frightened, then realized she could trust me, and began woefully recounting the horrors she had endured. She described how things people left with her for safekeeping were stolen from her cellar, how she had gone and gotten them back from the soldiers. She wept.

We rode back to Radivilov on a horse-drawn wagon. Seven or eight versts.[54] A moonlit night, snow-covered field, mild weather, tangled trees. So much silence, beauty and abundance. I talked with the coachman and he described what happened in Brody: "On Friday morning I harnessed the horses, was getting ready to leave for town; suddenly, I heard shooting. I ran inside the house. There was shouting, wailing. People went to hide wherever they could. I had left the horses outside, went to get them, and heard shooting again. I ran to a Pole's house and hid in the cellar with him. The fear was so awful that I wanted to die as fast as possible. And it was like that the whole day, while buildings were burning."

≈

At night, we were awoken by a commotion in the next room where an army quartermaster was staying. It seems he kidnapped a girl, drove her to Brody, and abandoned her somewhere, and from Brody he drove a girl back here. Now the mother of the abandoned girl is in his room demanding to know what he did with her, along with the girl that he brought here. The second girl burst into our room, crying hysterically. She is from Brody, has nothing on her and no way to get back. The hotel manager is taking it upon himself to bring her back to Brody. People say this officer is constantly causing debauchery of this kind here.

JANUARY 18

The train cars aren't here. Nor have we received any replies to the telegrams. We decided that Ratner should go to Kiev in case the *artel* worker sent a telegram there that says where he is held up.

I walk around the railway station several times a day and spend several hours there each time. Time and again you stumble upon scenes on the street, such as a drunken soldier being dragged past a building in a wheelbarrow, like a corpse. A crowd surrounds him. Some drunkards fly into fits of rage.

At night in the train station I met some officers from the Fifth Finland Infantry Regiment who were coming from Łomża province.[55] One of them recounted his impressions:

> There is of course a big difference between German and Austrian prisoners. The Germans are restrained, and if taken prisoner will nonetheless say, "we will still beat you!" Their defenses are all excellent. Their wire barriers are practically impassable; they're threaded with landmines. Touch it, and it explodes. Our trenches were three hundred paces from theirs. We could hear their conversations. Before their New Year, their envoy officer came to us and made a request: "Let us greet the New Year in peace, and we too will refrain from shooting at you on your New Year." Our superiors didn't let us enter into an agreement with them, but we didn't shoot at them. An officer of ours even sang "Baby Doll" for them. For that they didn't shoot at us on our New Year either. We rang in the New Year by singing "God Save the Tsar" three times.
>
> One time they fell on us in an attack and were beaten back. There were a lot of dead afterward. They requested permission to bury them. Our commanders refused and replied that they would bury them the next day. The Germans then asked for permission to send their own representative. After the dead Germans were buried and we gave them a military salute, a German lieutenant made a speech thanking his Russian comrades for the honor they had bestowed upon the Germans. "At your service!" they shouted at him.

At the train station I ran into a military doctor, Frumkin, who knows me. He was also stationed with the Fifth Finland regiment in Łomża province. He says that the troops' conduct toward the Jews is horrible, that they're like children who believe all kinds of tall tales. And the Jews are to blame because they sold vodka to the soldiers at a higher price. A Jew takes one additional kopek and then all Jews are guilty. But there were instances when officers gave out food to hungry populations, women, children.

≈

In the square across from the train station there are nearly four hundred Austrians who have been trampling in the cold for two hours now, waiting for a train. Russian soldiers are among them, chatting amiably and asking them questions. They are treating them in a most comradely manner. Some of the prisoners meekly joke about their situation: "We fought our share, now let others go and fight." "It's freezing, but at least further away from the shrapnel." One of them says something very funny in a lively and humorous way about an Austrian in the trenches, bursts into laughter, and the Russians who are standing behind him chuckle too. A tall, handsome soldier standing nearby folds his arms across his chest, observantly watches the crowd, and through clenched teeth, says "dee-fenders!" Here and there pale, crippled prisoners are begging: "Give me bread." Some give. One little soldier quips: "Why, isn't Franz Osipovich[56] feeding you well?"

At the edge of the blue-gray crowd a black stain emerges that blends with the bluish dusk into a single background. They are prisoners too; suspected persons who were taken neither as prisoners, nor as hostages. There are twenty-four Jews among them. Ragged, pale, scared. Young and old alike. They are shivering in the cold.

I walked over to them, began to ask them questions. Where are they from? From Laszki or Liszki. Why were they taken? They don't know. To where are they being taken? They don't know that either. At this moment they only know one thing—they are cold and hungry.

The guards began putting them on the train cars. For the Jews, a special car. But it seems the car was unheated. And it is seven or eight degrees below zero.[57] Even the gendarme sympathized: "Poor things, how will they make it?" The way these prisoners were placed in the wagons made for a particularly tragic scene. Steps for climbing up into a freight car do not exist. The soldiers clamber up easily by themselves and help some people get seated. But this was something terrible. Two or three men already in the wagon are feebly hoisting up the next man like a dead, inert body, who is barely hanging on, moaning. And the men below are propping him up just as lamely. Such frailty, clumsiness, ineptitude. Finally, with pains, moans and wails, and with the help of the Russian soldiers, they made it in.

"*Wielki Pan, proszę, trochę ugol.*"[58] An appeal rings out from the wagon, addressed to anyone who is walking past. The gendarme promises to give them some coal.

I am standing next to the wagon and can't help the unfortunate people in any way. I give them several rubles, tell them that I too am a Jew. Then one of them flings himself at me with a plea: "Do you know a doctor here? Have pity! My father here in the wagon is eighty-two years old and went blind five years ago. He is ill from traveling and the cold, and he is dying."

Why did they drag off an elderly, blind eighty-two year-old man?

I can't help them at all.

JANUARY 19

There are two traveling salesmen in the hotel. One of them saw me at a lecture somewhere, recognized me, introduced himself. He's a cultured man it seems. He's from Łódź. He owns a business there, and he abandoned it and fled. He was living in Kremenets most recently. He says that here and in the vicinity, relations between Jews and Poles are very peaceful, friendly. There is no Polish money, and they have to go to the Jews.

He explained the pogroms in Radivilov and Brody with utterly unusual reasons. At the very start of the war, Galician agitators appeared in villages near the Russian border and began inciting the peasants to seize land from the owners. Wherever those agitators went, robberies occurred. In Brody, the Austrians apparently hanged eighteen of those agitators and drove the rest away themselves.

JANUARY 20

Telegrams about the location of the train cars have come in at last. They passed Zdolbunov. This means they are stuck somewhere between Zdolbunov and Radivilov. Ratner returned from Kiev. There were no telegrams from the *artel* man there. But he was told in which of several stations the train cars ought to be. Tomorrow I'll go from station to station in search of them.

≈

At night I was at the train station with Ratner, talking about our mutual acquaintances. Suddenly, Kostia Rabinovich appeared at the entrance, saw me, and burst into laughter from surprise. He is a doctor with the Sixth Finland Infantry Regiment and is traveling with an echelon. I was happy to see him, as if he were family. He said many interesting things. He too of course talked about the widespread growth of antisemitism in the army and beliefs in Jewish espionage. There is no proof. There are rumors. An officer comes by: "In Warsaw we uncovered a mass of espionage organizations." And no one doubts they are Jewish.

He says there was a military circular: when military forces are being deployed, among the Jews who escort fellow Jews there may be persons who inspect what is being transported and to where, as well as which divisions are passing through; thus Jews are forbidden from accompanying departing forces.

He described the following, curious episode. Their division was stationed in trenches near Angerburg, in eastern Prussia. Several days before Christmas, an officer emerged from the German trenches with a white flag. He paused, waited. Ours saw him and sent out an officer and two soldiers with rifles to meet him.

They gathered and attempted to converse, but ours knew no German, nor the other any Russian. He understood only that the matter concerned the holidays and our side not shooting on those days. Using gestures and pointing to his watch, the German indicated he would return the following day at the same time for a reply. From the trenches they telephoned headquarters to inquire. From there they received the reply that they were not permitted to enter into any sort of official negotiations with the Germans, but could meet with the officer the following day to find out what he wanted. However, it seems not a single officer in the division knew any German. At that point, Rabinovich offered his services. The next day he set out for the trenches before dawn and climbed down into the bunker in which the battalion commander was stationed. Exactly two hours later an orderly informed them that a German officer was walking with two soldiers along the road that ran perpendicular to the trenches. Rabinovich went out to him with a soldier. They met halfway. The German officer sent one of his soldiers back. They came together and introduced themselves:

> "Lieutenant Koch."
> "Doctor Rabinovich."
> They shook hands.
> "What is the issue?"
> "Though we are indeed enemies," the lieutenant began, "it isn't personal. And we would like to propose that you allow us to spend the two days of the holiday in peace. For our part, we also promise not to shoot at you during your holiday."
> "I'm not authorized to give any kind of definitive promises," replied Rabinovich, "but as far as I know, it has been decided that we will not shoot during the holiday."

Rabinovich continued:

After that we began a personal conversation. He offered me a cigar; I offered him a cigarette. We lit them. I asked where he was from.
> "From Berlin," he replied.
> "I studied in Berlin."
> "I have a wife and child," he said.
> "So do I."
> "I'll send this flag to my wife as a memento . . . I'd like to give you something as a memento, but I don't have anything . . ."
> He fished around in his pocket, found a lighter and gave it to me. I couldn't give him anything; I had nothing on me. Then he invited us to their Christmas party.
> "We'll blindfold you and bring you over. You'll spend a wonderful evening with us. Then we'll bring you back."
> I promised to pass on his invitation. I must confess I had a burning desire to spend time with them. But we weren't allowed.
> Then Koch asked, "Is there anything you need?"
> "Thank you, we have everything. Anything you need?"
> "I would be very grateful if you could send me some Russian tea. I'm accustomed to drinking good tea."
> I promised.
> "Will the war be over soon?" he asked.
> "What do you think?"
> "It might end by the spring. The English aren't worth much as soldiers—the French even less. But your side won't back down. We may be fighting you for a long time."
> "But what will you fight with? You have no soldiers."

"We have plenty of soldiers!" he laughed. "I have two brothers—one in reserves, one still a youth—neither has been called up yet. Where did you hear that we have no soldiers?"

"That's printed in the papers."

"Well, the papers!"

"No, our newspapers don't lie. We have the ability to confirm announcements from the High Command, and it's remarkable how accurate they are. But your newspapers often exaggerate."

"Well, here, read them," he replied, and handed me a packet of German papers.

I gave him a packet of our announcements. We shook hands and parted. I was off duty the next day, but instructed our replacements to bring tea and a bottle of cognac to the meeting. The officer brought us champagne and candy.

At night there was another scandal in the hotel. A traveling salesman bought four hundred pieces of leather from a local Jew who had brought them over from Galicia. He gave a deposit. A police officer came by and demanded to see the salesman's permit. He didn't have one. Then the leather merchant suggested that the salesman give the policeman a fifty-ruble bribe. The salesman refused. The leather merchant won't budge. He has papers that give him the right to travel around the front because he works as a spy for the army, and he doesn't hide this, but even brags about it.

JANUARY 21

I left to look for the train cars. Along the way I talked with a Radivilov Jew. He spoke about the leather merchant, said that in the shtetl he was known as a shifty guy. His father and brother broke off ties with him. Now he's somebody—he makes deals, has put away tens of thousands of rubles. His father and brother were suspected of supplying animal fodder to the Austrians and taken under arrest. He intervened on their behalf and had their sentences commuted.

In Radivilov a factory owner, Liberman, was arrested on the charge of signaling to the enemy. When his house caught fire, he went to the water tower to extinguish it, and while doing so either lit something or sounded an alarm, I'm not exactly sure. But he was suspected and banished (?).

≈

I searched for the train cars at every station, and finally found them in Ozerny. They've been standing here for the past three days without moving. I pestered the station manager, and he promised to hook them to the transport train at night. In order to avoid sitting in that desolate station until nightfall I left for Zdolbunov. I spent about three hours there and thought I would stay the night, but didn't find a room. The shtetl is overflowing with troops. All of the shops along the street that leads from the station are completely packed. At about seven o'clock I left to go back, assuming I would spend the night in Dubno, where the trip usually takes an hour and a half. But this time I got to Dubno at four o'clock in the morning. The train cars are still in Ozerny. I was advised to stay in Dubno to claim them there.

JANUARY 22

From four in the morning on I languished at the tiny station, where there was neither space to lie down, nor even to sit. At the station there is a Countess Shuvalova Meal Station that serves the town, but it doesn't open until eight o'clock. In the waiting area a group of priests is discussing the origins of the word *zhid*. One says it comes from [illegible], others say Judas. But the conversation is academic. At eight o'clock, I had coffee at the meal station. A young lieutenant who was traveling with an echelon walked in. He began complaining:

> Being at the front is better than traveling with an echelon. On the road the men get sick. I now have two with typhus whom I've taken into my own compartment. But as soon as we reach a town no one is sick; they leave for town, get drunk on denatured alcohol, then come back and cause a riot. We've been here now for two days. They showed up today: "Give us firewood or we'll tear apart the train station." Well of course you can rein them in, even pull a revolver, but I don't forget that I'll have to be with them at the front. There was one time that I snapped at them. They settled down. But when I walked across the train car, behind me I heard: "Well, just wait, we'll be at the front—and the first bullet is for you." And such things have happened. My soldiers aren't novices. All of them were wounded and are coming back to the war.

≈

During the day, I saw those soldiers. Echelons were coming through the station one after another. The soldiers on the delayed trains came down

Русскіе войска у Львовскаго вокзала.

FIGURE 1.2. Russian troops at the main railroad station in Lvov, 1915. Ihor Kotlobulatov Collection. *Courtesy of the Center for Urban History of East Central Europe, L'viv.*

onto the platform with the novices and endless discussions ensued. They stood around in groups the whole day. Seasoned soldiers talked about combat, about the Austrians, and the newbies listened to them with greedy attention. A small, elderly soldier with a strikingly woeful, honest face and the expression of a diligent pupil pointedly imprinted himself in my memory. He stood holding both ends of a scarf that was wrapped around his neck, and a tall, young fellow with a round, naive, joyful face, wearing a "gift" shirt was staring at the storyteller. In a melodic and distinctly peasant style, he told stories about how the bullets were wheezing, how one nipped his foot, how with a small mounted patrol he once attacked a transport, and Germans scattered because they thought we were "with our family." And he joyfully concluded: "It's good to be at war! No structure at all—freedom. Pick a comfortable spot and lie right down!"

I rode into town to have a meal. A young boy who was selling newspapers got onto the sledge. I asked him if he was a Jew. He said he was a

Jew. And he instantly says in Yiddish to the driver, also a boy: "It's a shame I didn't say I'm a Russian. Then he would've paid for me."

≈

I stopped by an estate owned by a count to see the assistant there, Gelbort, who I met during the expedition. An exceptionally good man. He was terribly happy to see me. He described how a Jewish committee was established at the start of the war that delivered bread and milk to the train station for the wounded. And what happened? The gendarmes and railroad administration chased off the Jews, saying they were meddling too much.

Gelbort was in Radivilov at the time it was destroyed. Everyone sat in hiding—there was nowhere to go, although he did go out at night. Suddenly, a Jew came over to him and asked—begged—him to come to his place. He was observing a *yahrtzeit*[59] and in need of a tenth man for prayers.[60] He went. After the prayers, the man then called them outside to bless the moon.[61] The shops are being looted. But this man's only concern is to bless the moon. And so they went.

This morning there was a small pogrom here. The soldiers in the echelon of that officer I met at the meal station robbed the merchants of all their goods.

≈

I spent the whole day dealing with the railway station director and commandant until I managed to retrieve the train cars from Ozerny. And it took an equal amount of effort before I was able to get the cars hooked to a transport train leaving for Brody. I boarded that train myself at eight o'clock and arrived in Radivilov at half past three in the morning.

JANUARY 23

I woke Ratner and we packed our things and set off for Brody. We left our repulsive companions behind in Radivilov. Their train cars are still in Dubno. We arrived in Brody at seven o'clock in the morning. There were no wagon drivers. We walked along the empty street. A long chain

of burned houses stood out starkly against the backdrop of that deso-
lation. A small, squat house stood out among them, strangely intact.
Now an old Jew with a blanket wrapped around his shoulders stood
next to that house and hopelessly, miserably stared ahead. When we
approached him he offered us a low bow. I talked with him, gave him
some coins—and he followed us with a long, shocked stare.

A few hours later when we walked along the street and stopped next
to a shop, we were mobbed by poor children. A tiny, strange sight appeared among them—an old lady with disheveled gray hair. Elbowing
her way forward and staring at us with the eyes of a hungry dog, she
suddenly sang out in Russian, "ca-na-ry birdy!"—some ballad about a
little bird that alighted and flew away and took love with itself. It was
rather hard to follow the point of the song, but every one of the words
grated on the ears. It was agonizing to listen to that crazy old woman's
raspy, woeful song as she closed in on us, her eyes fixed on us, apparently in the hope of astounding us with her knowledge of a Russian
song. The children were howling with laughter. We gave her some change
and quickly left. And like a nightmare, that awful song about the "canary
birdy" haunted us the whole day.

≈

More trouble with the train cars. They need to be transferred here to
Austrian cars that are built for Austrian tracks, which have a narrower
gauge. But there are no train cars. And we don't know when there will
be. The intensified transport of troops and artillery prohibits the use of
train cars for any other types of freight. We therefore decided to go to
Lvov to speak with the Zemstvo Union and get their advice about ob-
taining train cars.

I had gone through so much before receiving permission to travel to
Galicia, that I still didn't fully trust that with my papers I would be admitted to Lvov without further difficulties. On top of that, various
rumors had been going around. People said that Jews weren't getting
through under any circumstances, that special permits were required.
In Kiev, I heard that D. F. Fainberg[62] was refused a permit—and he had
a personal letter for Bobrinskii's[63] vice-regent from his brother. And
I boarded the train with a sense of anxiety. However, everything went

very smoothly. The commandant quickly glanced at my paper while passing through, and handed it back to me without saying anything.

The road to Lvov doesn't present anything of interest. There were no battles here, and anything that happened over these past five months was smoothed over with time and snow. Only the approach to Lvov is interesting. The locale is strikingly beautiful: a whole chain of large hills and mountains surrounds the city. It gives the impression of being a naturally fortified, impregnable fortress. How the Austrians surrendered the city without a fight is incomprehensible.

There are officers in the train car, of course. Endless stories. An officer tells of the following instance:

> An ensign officer commanded an attack under deadly fire and charged ahead. Just two or three soldiers ran after him. He started calling the others; they wouldn't go. Then he yelled at them: "At least, scream 'hurrah!'" and threw himself ahead with his two comrades. They were killed, of course. In general, the young officers display astounding bravery, and have to be restrained. The soldiers display great courage too. But only when their superiors are present. They become helpless and confused the instant their commanders are killed and they're left alone. Sometimes you have to force them into combat with a revolver in hand.
>
> The Germans fight savagely. Our side captured some trenches. Two officers remained there. They wouldn't surrender, were shooting. It was a shame to kill them. Their hands were tied up. They kept biting, spitting in our faces until they were tied up and driven away.
>
> The officer judged the conduct of the Cossacks very critically. They steal and kill prisoners. The Caucasian "Wild Division"[64] is particularly known for this. If you ask them, "did you take a lot of prisoners?" they say, "Why take prisoners? Sekir bashka!"[65] One of the wounded was in a hospital. He had a saber covered in dried blood and was very proud of it.
>
> The soldiers grew so accustomed to bombs that they hardly noticed them. They were stationed near the Dunajec River. Whenever a bomb landed in the water, it was a holiday for the soldiers. Fish soup! The explosions stunned the fish and they floated to the surface. The soldiers collected them and cooked fish soup.

The [Lvov] train station is enormous, magnificent, spacious, with artistic architecture. I don't know of any like it in Russia.

Lvov was captured so simply and without fanfare that somehow you didn't get the impression the victory had been a genuine one. And I couldn't get a good sense of the city's grandeur. But nonetheless, this is a proper capital city, reminiscent of Kiev or Warsaw. Big buildings.

FIGURE 1.3. Karl Ludwig Street, Lvov (now Svobody Prospekt), the city's main street. Local civilians walk alongside Russian military forces on horseback. George Grantham Bain Collection. *Courtesy of the Library of Congress.*

Wide streets, lavish shops, old castles and churches, monuments. A big European city. From the outside it looks lively. But there isn't a single cab. Two trams are running, Austrian conductors are driving them, Austrian policemen are here and there. They are courteous and deferentially polite. The masses are overwhelmingly Jewish, with long *peyes.*[66]

A large crowd is standing near a building in anticipation that bread will be distributed.

I went to the Cracow Hotel for dinner. There was a mass of officers; a remarkably beautiful, recently renovated restaurant. The cooks and servers are from Moscow. You could have imagined you'd come to the

Praga,[67] but the food was rather bad. Time and again you stumble upon signs written in Russian or a Russian shop.

There are icons displayed in many windows. This is also the case in Brody and throughout all of Galicia. A rather sinister omen.

~

At the Union of Zemstvos they couldn't tell us anything about train cars. We stopped by the Gentry Organization.[68] There they treated us very considerately, expressed a willingness to help. The Gentry Organization has a hospital train that makes trips between Brody and Tarnów almost every day. And they'll allow us to transfer our things onto the cars of the first hospital train, which they'll send to Brody. With this it seems our troubles should come to an end. We returned to Brody in the evening.

JANUARY 24

In the morning I went to the synagogue. The synagogue is historic, four hundred to five hundred years old, they say. It is rich with silver implements: the Torah crown, scroll handles, ark, curtains, light fixtures are all very antique, valuable. And no one thinks of selling them to feed the hungry. They are "eternal." I entered the small chapel. People there were praying very passionately, swaying from side to side. They pointed out an elderly man to me who was standing motionless in a corner, and whispered that this was "the *Rebbe*." One of the congregants began describing to me how the town had suffered. Five synagogues burned down, as well as hundreds of houses.

"Do you see that Jew over there?" he pointed out to me, "he was a mailman. Just as you see him, with long *peyes*, he used to deliver letters, was considered a government worker, earned a living. And now he's dying of hunger."

I visited Dr. Kalakh. Two others were visiting him. The second one recounted the following:

On August 14[69] we heard cannonade fourteen kilometers in the distance. Within half of an hour, the Austrian troops left the city. It was quiet for two hours. At half past nine, one Cossack appeared and asked where the postal building was located, and galloped off straight away. Another Cossack appeared right after that, and five minutes later shooting began all of a sudden and lasted for three-quarters of an hour. Then it died down. Of course, everyone sat in hiding. When it was quiet we tried to get a look outside. There wasn't a Russian soul in sight. At about half past eleven, I went outside. All of a sudden, I heard a bomb blast, then another, hitting the Prague Bank. Seven or eight shots were fired but nobody was hurt. We went to hide in the cemetery. Cossacks appeared there out of the blue. They saw us but didn't do anything to us. They asked us for water. But they made us drink some of it first to make sure it wasn't poisoned. Then they left. Two or three hours later they left and didn't come back for eight days.

When we recovered a bit, we found out what happened. When the Cossacks entered the town, there were shots fired from one street that killed the Cossack commander. The Cossacks started shooting. Just then at the Polish Hotel, the hotel owner's daughter, Kharash, became frightened by the shooting and jumped from a window. The Cossacks decided that it was she who fired the shots and they skewered her on the spot, tore her to pieces. The father of that girl was sitting in jail—the Austrians imprisoned him as a Russian spy. When the Russians occupied Brody they released him, but later arrested him again and deported him to Russia. The following people were killed at the time of the shooting: 1) Kharash's daughter; 2) Reif; 3) Flig—his wife became sick and died; 4) Another person died in a fire; 5) The teacher, Golembovskaia, a Christian; 6) Katz, a young man, was wounded.

At half past seven on August 23, the Cossacks came back and set fire to the postal building and a few houses. The fires were extinguished. Then at half past ten, they began shoving sulfured lances through windows and torching one house after another. Because of the strong wind, the whole neighborhood burned down. And it was then that the town's shops and trading stalls were looted. One week later on September 1, a soldier broke into a garden and started stealing apples. The owner threw him out. He fired a shot. Then the soldiers set fire to that house and forbade it from being extinguished. They fired shots for a while after that but no one was killed. Since then it has been quiet. Yes, on the 23rd, when the Russians entered the city, the locals greeted them with bread and salt. After that life began to return to its routine. However, different shops are repeatedly robbed. The inhabitants have been forbidden from leaving their homes after eight o'clock at night, and thieves can freely loot the shops. Now there is a different menace. Time and again, dozens of families will be expelled from various houses within the span of a few hours, because the building is needed for a hospital or some another institution.

Later in the day, I saw an unusual scene in the street. A Jewish dray-man was driving a large cart filled with household wares, and a Jew and Jewess were walking behind him. And this was the Sabbath. They were expelled a few hours ago and are searching for shelter. The doctor recounted how all the elderly people had been expelled from the old age

FIGURE 1.4. Expelled Jews, Galicia, 1915. Bernard Bardach Collection. *Courtesy of the Leo Baeck Institute, New York.*

home in the same way, because the Russians apparently needed it for some reason. He, the doctor, had to bring thirty-eight elderly people to his hospital.

There were formerly eighteen thousand inhabitants living in Brody, three-quarters of them Jews, the rest Ruthenians. There are now nearly five thousand Jews left; among them many are from neighboring shtetls. Anyone with the least bit of wealth ran away. Those who are left were robbed, ruined. Everyone is poor. They received 500 rubles in aid from Samuil Mess for firewood. But this is a drop in a sea.

The first military commandant was a man named Chertkov. After him there was Kulchitskii. Because there was no mayor, he ordered everyone to assemble and elect a new one. The people came together. They waited for him; he doesn't show up. They waited for him for three hours and dispersed. Several Russophiles stayed behind and elected themselves—you will be the mayor, I will be this, another will be that. In this way, one Kushpet, formerly the butcher, became the mayor. He's a shrewd man—changed his tune right away, declared himself a Russophile, converted to Orthodoxy. He calls the shots in the city.

There were various Jewish communal institutions, a Talmud Torah,[70] Lekhem Evyonim.[71] The kahal[72] manages all of it. Now the kahal no longer officially exists. And no one thinks it is beneficial to raise this question. The hospital was sustained by revenues from the bathhouse and the sale of kosher meat. Now the mayor has taken all of that away. After great effort, Dr. Kalakh managed to obtain a lease from the mayor for these institutions for 400 crowns per year. Raise your voice the slightest bit with the mayor and he threatens "expulsion to Kiev." The saddest thing is that the schools are closed, the children run around with nothing to do, asking for handouts and acting like hooligans.

I gave the doctor several rubles to distribute to the poor.

JANUARY 25

The Zemstvo Organization's[73] hospital train hasn't arrived. We are expecting it at any moment and inquire at the train station in the meantime. A former bonded warehouse there was converted into an evacuation point. A huge, endless space is completely filled with the wounded arriving from the Carpathians, up to three thousand every day. They feed them here, bandage them, and send them to Russia in Russian train cars. The work is remarkably thorough and efficient.

I met two doctors who are working at the evacuation site, Cherkeskii and Gordon, both Jews. They've worked here for many long months. Cherkeskii told me many interesting things. Evlogii[74] terrorized the Ruthenian population here. The [Russians] don't forcibly convert them, but they make it clear that without ties to Orthodoxy, they shouldn't hope for any kind of favors, while those who convert will receive every kindness. The doctor was taking his meals at the home of a Ruthenian woman. One time he came by and found she was horribly worried and had hidden her children. She was told the children would be taken away by force and converted to Orthodoxy. This is an indication of the atmosphere.

According to the version the doctor heard, the destruction of Brody began when a Cossack *esaul*[75] went after a Jewish girl. A resident in her building, a Pole, shot at him. The Pole managed to escape but the girl was killed. Then the [Cossacks] left the city limits and fired two rounds into the city. After that they doused the buildings in kerosene and set them on fire. The doctor has been here from the very start. At first the population was extremely frightened—respected elderly men would bow to the ground before anyone in the army. The soldiers tore at the Jews' side locks, broke into houses, acted savagely. The doctor is living in a small house that belongs to a large estate near the railroad station. That estate and its residence belonged to a millionaire, Shmidt, who fled before the arrival of the Russians. However, his huge estate remained unoccupied for a long time. Some sort of connections were protecting his house and the estate. And at that time in the city, when fifty families at once were being expelled with six to twelve hours' notice, his properties were not touched. Finally, the office building was occupied. But an order to clear out was instantly received. However, it was occupied on the order of a higher authority and they're not clearing out. As for the residence itself, the doctor still doesn't know what is happening.

Relations between Poles and Jews were not good. Initially the commanders here acted obnoxiously. Like all heroes in the rear they were braggarts. They incited agitation against Jews. They told the Ruthenians, "Here the Jews are the bosses, but by us they get it like so!" and drew their hands across their necks.

JANUARY 26

The hospital train isn't here, but the *artel* worker found empty cars at the station that belong to the Gentry Organization, and we transferred our cars onto them. Tonight they'll be hooked to the train and sent to Lvov. We'll leave tomorrow morning too.

Ratner worked by himself today. I was lying in bed. Yesterday I caught a bad cold.

JANUARY 27

I drove to the train station with an elderly drayman. We talked for a while.

> I have three sons, and all of them are at war, and I don't know where they are or how they are. I worried my whole life—never ate my fill, never slept late, only so as to help them on in life—and now in my old age I'm alone. You ask what is happening in the city? People are dying of hunger. There were great rich men here and they all fled. They left and took their hard cash with them—and left the paupers to starve to death. What kind of man is Dr. Kalakh? He's a drunkard, thinks of no one but himself. He stayed because he's afraid his house will be requisitioned.

Lvov.[76] We arrived at five o'clock. We were promised that our train cars would be hooked to the echelon tomorrow morning. At night, I sought out Diamand,[77] one of the community activists and a member of the kahal. He later confessed that my arrival frightened him. Someone came to tell him: "An officer has come." "Not again!" he thought. He's been through a lot. He informed me that D. F. Fainberg was here and had a meeting with Bobrinskii that left him very pleased, after the latter promised a certain amount of money for the poor. Since then, Dr. Lander[78] came and visited several locations; Dr. Shabad[79] as well. Here in general is what happened in Lvov.

When the Russians arrived they appointed Sheremetev[80] as the military governor—a very good, cultured, and kind man, in Diamand's opinion. He put the civilian population at ease, and life began to return to a routine, insofar as that was possible. They took hostages right away, and Diamand was among them. But Sheremetev freed them three days later. Sheremetev praised Diamand after learning that of thirty people in the Jewish kahal, he alone had stayed. Then Sheremetev left and Eikhe[81] was appointed to be the governor. Shortly after his appointment, on a Sunday, two days before Yom Kippur,[82] shooting began all of a sudden in the city. People later said a Jew fired the first shot—there were even witnesses, although each of them saw the shooting Jew on a different street. After the shooting, there were eighteen dead Jews,[83] all of them poor people. The Jews, reeling from horror, were afraid to leave their houses on Yom Kippur and didn't go to Kol Nidrei[84] at night. Jewish soldiers who wanted to pray and found the synagogues boarded up went off to see the Commandant to request that he open the synagogues for them. The deputy governor (?) was informed of this and sent out a car to the rabbi, with a request that he drive over. The rabbi replied that it was forbidden by Jewish law to drive on Yom Kippur and went on foot. The deputy governor (?) asked him what sense there was in the Jews' demonstrating by not going to pray. The rabbi replied that this was not at all a demonstration, but simply the fact that Jews feared another shooting. The deputy governor (?) then assuaged them and placed guards next to the synagogues, and the following day the Jews (albeit not everyone) went to pray.

After the shooting, hostages were taken again, and Diamand was among them, and once again, they were quickly released. A few weeks ago he and a several others were taken again for unknown reasons, but later released with the requirement that they make an appearance twice a week.

In a city of two hundred thousand residents, there were more than sixty thousand Jews.[85] Many of the richest and most affluent people fled. And even with Lvov being flooded with refugees from surrounding towns and shtetls, there are just 50,000 people left.

The gemina/kahal[86] still exists and is functioning, but it has very few resources since its principal sources of income dried up, and it hasn't been able to adopt any measures to properly organize aid for hungry people. Since the start of mobilization, bread rations (one kilogram twice a week) were distributed, mainly to the wives of reservists, 1,700

FIGURE 1.5. Herman Diamand.
*Courtesy of National Digital
Archive, Poland.*

of them; now their number has increased to 2,000. Among the organizations in the city there are forty-five soup kitchens, including five kosher ones for Jews. This is all that is happening at the moment. In the city there are twelve gymnasiums, three *realschules*,[87] a polytechnic university, and numerous national schools. All of them were closed. A public school is now ready to be opened, under the condition that Russian language is taught there five times a week. The courts are still open and functional. The homes of people who fled are being requisitioned. An order was issued in regard to their stores. Those that were not opened by a certain date would be requisitioned. Family members opened them.

≈

In regard to civic relations:

Prior to 1868, their government was a German one; Jews, who supported the government, were opposed by the Poles.[88] In 1868, the government passed into the hands of the Poles, and the Jews backed the Poles. Good relations developed between the two groups; moreover, the Jews proved to be a good electoral base for the Poles. An attempt at a boycott failed. For this reason, the Ruthenian intelligentsia opposes the Jews.

The governor in Tarnopol, Chartoryzhskii, issued an order that neither Jews nor Catholics are allowed to work in the courts.

There are many raped, pregnant girls in the shtetls.

JANUARY 28

We had hoped that our train cars would be hooked to a transport train this morning, but they weren't. And we continue to wait for the Gentry Organization's hospital train, which is supposed to return from Brody.

Yesterday I arranged with Diamand that I would visit the gemina if I didn't leave. I went there in the morning. It's a big, very nicely furnished space, almost as fine as that of the Warsaw gemina. There was a huge portrait of Franz Joseph; portraits of rabbis.

"The Orthodox poisoned that one."[89] One of the portraits, a young man with a strikingly intelligent face, was pointed out to me.

Diamand wasn't there. In the room where I sat to wait for him, there was a gentleman with whom I talked for a while. He is apparently a Jewish deputy to Parliament from (I forgot his name). Diamand arrived soon afterward, and was followed by a rabbi, Dr. Hausner,[90] a young man, thirty-two or thirty-three years old, with a very wise, intelligent face. He spoke about the meetings he had held with Count Bobrinskii, both on his own and together with D. F. Fainberg. He recounted his conversation with the count—and his responses were so smart, tactful and quick-witted that I was simply struck. I won't transcribe the conversation because Fainberg has it written down verbatim. In their discussion, they recalled Herzl,[91] who they had both personally known. After the Dreyfus Affair,[92] Herzl fell to thinking about the Jewish Question and began saying that Jews needed their own territory. One time, while sitting with Güdemann,[93] he unfolded a map and began searching for a territory for Jews on it.

"You are looking in the wrong place—look here!" Güdemann told him, and pointed to Palestine.

FIGURE 1.6. Bernard Hausner, wearing the uniform of an Austro-Hungarian Army officer. Photograph taken during World War I. *Courtesy of Tami Hausner Raveh.*

Herzl tried to convert Tsadok ha-Kohen[94] to Zionism but didn't succeed. When he was asked about the outcome of their discussions, he fluttered his hand and said, *"nisht keyn Tsadok!"*[95]

They also spoke about Mathias Acher[96] and Zhitlowsky.[97] Hausner had met the latter in Palestine. "A centrifugal mind," is how Hausner defined him.

≈

In the evening, Ratner and I went to visit Hausner. He spoke at length about the things he endured over the past several months, about horrors that took place, especially in the remote shtetls. In the shtetl of Buczacz, forty girls were raped. He recounted how on the Sabbath of Repentance[98] he wept bitterly during the prayers. After the prayers a Jewish soldier approached him: *"Rebbe,* why were you crying like that?"

"Aren't there things to cry about?"

"Don't cry, *Rebbe.* We Jewish soldiers, 200,000 of us, won't let anyone hurt you."

The soldier's naivety and wish to console him were very touching. Alongside this story the rabbi recounted something whose nightmarish horror was staggering. He was called to a hospital to see a dying Jewish soldier: "He's requesting a rabbi." Hausner went and found the wounded man in a terrible state. The wounded man looked at him and said, *"Rebbe,* I can't die."

"What's the matter? Why not?"

"I don't know."

"Maybe you have some kind of sin weighing on your soul?"

He was silent. He then asked for everyone to step away. It was just the two of them. Then he began:

"Rebbe, we came to a shtetl. The soldiers were breaking into houses and stealing. I ran inside one house too. There was an old man there, a *dayan.*[99] I screamed, 'give me money!' and started snatching at some of the old man's things. The old man didn't give in and started fighting back."

He fell silent and did not continue for some time.

"Well, what did you do?"

"I killed him—stabbed him with a bayonet . . ."

The rabbi recoiled from him in horror. And the dying man wept.

"How could you raise your hand to kill a defenseless person, a Jew, a *dayan*, an old man?"

He wept silently and then whispered, "Is there any way for me to repent, tell me?"

"I don't know . . ." the rabbi replied. "I'll think about it. I'll come back in the afternoon."

When he returned that afternoon the soldier was already dead.

We sat at the station the whole night until very late. We were promised that our train cars would be hooked to one train, then to a different one, and finally to the Gentry Organization's hospital train. Finally, at midnight, when the orders were given to connect the cars, it turned out that earlier this morning they were sent with a freight train straight to Dębica.[100] Now we just have to follow them. We'll take the Gentry Organization train.

I sat inside the station the whole time I wasn't running around to deal with the train cars. I met some officers. As a gift, one gave me an Austrian proclamation in which it is reported that soldiers are promised seven rubles in exchange for a Russian weapon and one kopek for a cartridge, and that prisoners in Austria are well fed and maintained. In relation to this subject he told me the following:

These proclamations are posted on sticks in front of our trenches, and to tempt our soldiers over to their side they'll tie on an undershirt or some other piece of finery. Our men laugh at this, of course. By the way, we put up exactly the same proclamations. We had the following situation: a number of Serbs came to us and surrendered. One says, "We have to send for our comrades. Hang on, give me a pen and ink and I'll write to them." He sat down and wrote a long letter—he listed all of his comrades by name, described the joys of Russian prison for them. He suggested that a soldier deliver the letter. He recounted for him in detail how to get there, where to find the passage through the wire fence, how to climb into the trench, where to leave the letter. They found a daredevil, and he crawled over, placed the letter in the designated spot, and came back. The Serb asked him: "Did you catch a whiff of anything while you were crawling through the trench?" "Why yes I did, there was a stench coming from the right." "Well, well, there is indeed. That place is to the right. That means you went the right way." The following night, all forty Serbs came to us and surrendered.

JANUARY 29

We left at two o'clock in the morning. In the first-class compartments there were either no seats, or they didn't want to give them to us. We were led to a spot in a fourth-class car that was unheated and crammed full of mattresses. It was as cold as it was outside. I laid down in a waistcoat and covered myself in my overcoat and a blanket, but it was still cold. On top of that, I had caught a bad cold and found it hard to breathe—definitely an asthma attack. In the morning some officer from an Automobile Company took a seat. He was full of spite and irritated. He cursed the generals, called all of them third-rate.

"Russia has three enemies: lice, the Germans, and our generals."

He said that Rennenkampf is being held inside the Peter and Paul Fortress. He told the old tale of how one time at a military council, the Grand Duke suggested they surrender Warsaw without a fight, and all of the generals agreed with him. Only Ivanov[101] (or Ruzskii[102]) said that if they surrendered Warsaw, he would put a bullet through his head. As everyone was leaving the Grand Duke held him back: "Wait a minute." And he ordered him to call up all the reserves at the last minute and not to surrender Warsaw. The Germans immediately found out about all of this from the generals they had bribed. Therefore, they headed for Warsaw at full speed. And stumbled upon us.

≈

People say there is a directive that Austrians who are taken prisoner on whom explosive shells are found are to be shot.

≈

A Circassian is riding the train. He has three valuable coats. People ask, "where did you get them?" "I bought them." "How much did you pay?" "Why pay? I paid nothing. They don't take prisoners, but they don't show any mercy—they gouge out their eyes, chop off their hands, and cut them loose." There were two Cossacks in the train compartment with us. One was thirty years old, the other about fifty, if not more. The first was headed to his division at the front, the second was traveling from the same *stanitsa*[103] just to accompany his landsman. The first was a typical brute—when speaking he sort of characteristically moves his head, nostrils, and lips. He speaks with a singsong voice. To him, the whole war comes down to bravery and vengeance. Nothing exists for him apart from his Cossack division or company or platoon—they are his family. All of them are from the same *stanitsa* and know each other by name. They drop the names Vas'ka Kozhur, Mikita Poliavko— all one of us, our folk. They stand solidly behind one another. And if one of them is killed, they will sorely avenge his death, without sparing anyone or anything.

He talks about politics too. He went to Russia to get treated for a woo-und, and liked the moo-ood. "Russia has displayed gre-eat apathy in this war."

"How so?" I marveled.

"Because everybody cares, as one, and does good things."

"What does that have to do with apathy?"

"What else? It's obvious, everyone acts in one spirit, all as one—and it's good."

Apparently he meant to say "empathy."

$$\approx$$

We passed Zholkva,[104] which seems to be the only city that escaped destruction. Rava-Ruska[105] was burned and destroyed. The train didn't stop there. But then the locomotive suddenly broke down at one of the next stations, in Oleszyce. Someone was dispatched to Rava for another locomotive, and we stood idle for about six hours. I went into the shtetl, which lay about two versts[106] from the station.

It's a small shtetl, with destroyed buildings here and there, but in the marketplace the trading stalls were open and there was brisk bargaining.

I stopped a Jewish boy and asked him where the rabbi lives. He showed me the way. As we walked, he told me that soldiers looted all of the shops here and raped two girls, the daughters of prominent business owners.

At the rabbi's house I found ten old men standing in another room praying *maariv*.[107] In the first room, the rabbi's mother was lying sick in bed, and his wife and someone who looked like his younger sister were sitting at a table with prayer books and praying as well. They were confused when they saw me, but after learning that I am a Jew they were completely at ease. They woefully recounted how everyone was ruined, how the poor were starving to death. Among the praying men there were two Palestinian Jews who had gotten stranded here. Shloyme Shrentsel, the *dayan*, came by. I spoke with him and left several rubles for the poor.

"Won't you leave something for Passover too?," he asked.

"Settle that here yourselves."

≈

At night we crossed a bridge over the San River[108] near Jarosław. We rode across a new bridge, swaying ever so slightly. Next to it there was another bridge that had been blown up. It was an enchanting picture. The whole bridge, the new one, was perfectly visible beneath the light of a projector. Here and there the clang of workers rang out, and in the depths below the rapid, noisy river was boiling amidst a heap of fallen beams and icy fragments. Even a few days ago, the trains hadn't used this bridge, but rather transferred the cars one by one on a cable. We passed Jarosław at three o'clock in the morning.

JANUARY 30

Our train reached Rzeszów,[109] where it received a telegram to return to Jarosław. We have to stay here until four o'clock in the morning to wait for a transport train. I am fine with this. The station is wrecked, falling apart. One of the few rooms that are attached to it was converted into a buffet where tea is served. The owner of the buffet is a Russian, from either Tula or Riazan, who had intended to go to Lvov but ended up here. There are four Ruthenian girls who used to work for the previous owner also at the counter. They are wearing rather fancy clothes and make a suspicious impression.

We took a room across from the station and brought over our things. Near the hotel there was a Jewish shop. I went inside, talked with people.

The city was big and affluent. There were more than ten thousand Jews living here. Now there are less than half of that number. Everyone with money fled.

The Russians arrived four months ago. All of the stores were looted. There was a large egg trade here, but all of the stocks were broken. The shop owner showed me the remnants of his wares, which were covered in paint. The Russians then left, the Austrians returned and remained in the city for four weeks, after which the Russians came back and have been here ever since.

There is neither a kahal, nor a rabbi, nor anyone who is paying attention to starving people. And there are a lot of them.

I walked into town. It's a large, beautiful European city with historic buildings. In most of the shops, the shades are pulled down and in a few of those the doors are boarded up. But there are no burnt buildings. In an enormous marketplace packed full of people from the villages, there is vigorous trading. There are several big cafés.

Here too there are icons in the windows, on the gates, and on the doors of all the Christian houses. A rather sinister omen.

≈

I went to the synagogue. It is old, made of stone, six hundred years old, they say. Inside it there are many valuable things—chandeliers, sconces, curtains. An old, bowed seventy-two-year-old rabbi's assistant greeted us in a modest and calm manner, like so many other assistants, and extended his hand.

In the chapel near the synagogue where we found him, there was nobody apart from ourselves.

"Right here," he began softly, "people used to learn Talmud day and night, and now there is no one. I have to run around looking for a minyan."[110]

"Did somebody hurt you?"

"They hurt everybody. . . . There are bad people among yours and ours both. Peace should come soon."

I gave him several rubles. He didn't even look at what I gave him or offer me thanks.

"I don't need anything any longer. I go around gathering things and give them to hungry people. There are so many hungry people here! I'll give out your charity too."

The old man gave the impression of being a truly holy person.

≈

While walking back from the synagogue, I stumbled upon an interest-ing scene. There were a number of mounted Cossacks escorting a large group of Austrian prisoners on foot across the market. They stopped for a brief time, and near a trading stall where a mass of them accumulated, screams rang out and several prisoners bolted and blended in to the crowd, which then moved on. I walked over to the stall. A young Jewess, the owner, stood there sobbing; a young man with a desperate look on his face stood next to her.

"What's the matter?"

"The prisoners came in, grabbed all my goods and ran away," replied the shop owner.

I gave her a ruble. And it proved to be a rather original scene: a man from the enemy camp came to help someone who was robbed by men from her own side, who were walking past as prisoners.

≈

I had a small package I had brought from Moscow for some civilian gen-eral, Viktorov, who runs a meal station here. I sought him out. He is liv-ing in a train car near the railroad station. He greeted Ratner and me very warmly, served us dinner. He described how he has worked here for the last three months distributing up to seven hundred meals a day, and this is insufficient. He is working with the town council to find resources to aid the population (this is all in regard to the Christian population alone). He is unhappy with the intensified Russification. He considers it a very cruel thing that the schools are closed. He and the local military commander hope to reopen them.

≈

A train carrying munitions on its way to Dębica appeared in the eve-ning. All of its compartments were the same class. One had broken windows and a missing wall. The lower ranks were sitting there. An-other had some sort of strange construction. Two officers, a medical orderly, and a nurse were sitting there. We squeezed in there too and were off.

The officer recounted how at the start of the war he read in military papers that the Austrians issued an order not to take prisoners. Of course, the intent of this was to keep our men from surrendering. But initially our side also tried to "take no prisoners."

More stories about the Wild Division. About twenty men went out on reconnaissance. They ran across a whole division. The Wild men told their officer: "Lead us into battle." "Have you all lost your minds?" "Lead us, it's nothing—we'll route them, wipe them out." He ignored them, of course. The men returned. They went to the colonel: "Give us a different officer. We don't want to go with this one. He's a coward."

≈

We arrived in Dębica at night. The train station was fairly large but there was no place to lie down. I could have gone to see the city; I'd heard the entire marketplace burned down. But it was dark, and there was an impenetrable mud that kept us from walking very far. Military units were occupying every building on the first street. One of the officers who was traveling with us learned of a lodging here for officers. I went with him, and we found it with some effort. It was a large room with two cots and two decrepit couches, with no linens. A doctor was sleeping on one of the cots. We asked him if there were bedbugs. "It's alright," he says, "I don't feel any at the moment."

We walked back to the train station. Our group removed stretchers for the wounded from a freight car, unfolded them, spread out in one of the rooms and laid down to sleep. The others also opted to sleep on the stretchers on the floor, rather than in the officers' room.

The officer with whom I walked made a rather strange impression. He had a stern, inquisitive gaze, a contemptuous face, tightly closed lips. He didn't say much. But when he did speak, he asked some naive questions.

He mentioned the following in passing:

"I used to be a skeptic, an atheist, even mocked religion. But when I read Tolstoy's pamphlet (I don't remember which one—S. A.) I became a believer. I have faith in God and pray every day . . ."

"But how do you combine Tolstoy with the war?"

"You shall see what people will become after the war. They will be reborn. It will be a different world."

JANUARY 31

I was woken up at three o'clock in the morning. A freight train is leaving for Wola Rzędzińska, the final station prior to Tarnów.[111] The train doesn't go any further because of shelling. Our train cars showed up in Dębica. We hooked them to the train and found room for ourselves in a freight car. It was cold and windy there, but I squeezed in between bags and slept soundly to Wola.

We arrived in Wola before sunrise. The horizon was burning, as if filled with blood. There were no wagons, of course, and after leaving our baggage in the train car we departed for Tarnów on foot (about seven or eight versts).[112] We could hear a cannonade. After walking almost three versts we spotted a peasant driving a wagon and rode the rest of the way with him.

≈

We didn't find Igor Platonovich Demidov; he had gone away somewhere. We visited the State Duma Hospital, met with the corps: the head nurse who manages the group together with Demidov is Countess Sofia Alekseevna Bobrinskaia, an older woman (an old maid it seems), who has a very unattractive, almost warped figure, and a very pretty face. There are many young people, younger than Countess Bobrinskaia, and medical orderlies, also from the nobility. They live simply, harmoniously, and work hard. They told me that without exception everyone on the staff must pass a lengthy initial trial, doing all types of menial work, down to cleaning the lavatory. Some ran away, but those who stayed on work remarkably well. Demidov is the soul of the detachment; he is fanatically devoted to the cause, a man who seems very interesting, a religious mystic.

Tarnów was shelled by forty-two centimeter guns earlier in January. For their work under fire, everyone on the staff was awarded with St. George's Crosses. They recounted that when a forty-two centimeter shell exploded in the city, Ordynskii, who was here at the time, fled the city on foot without saying goodbye, and took the list of the items he had delivered with him.

Demidov arrived in the evening. He's a young man, thirty-five or thirty-six years old;[113] is tall, thin, sturdy; has the enormous eyes of a zealot and a scruffy beard. There is something simple and peasant-like in his refined, aristocratic features. One of those faces that draws attention to itself.

He is serious, deep. He tries to be fair with everyone, is a man who works on himself. He greeted me very warmly. He made sure I wasn't in need of warm clothing or tobacco. I do need linens, rolling papers, soap, candles, matches, liniment, and most of all, boots.

The city survived the bombing, fortunately. It is a big European city that resembles our provincial cities. There are large government and private buildings, historic buildings, a synagogue, Catholic Church, town hall, and monuments. There were factories, mills, and tailor workshops, where as many as three hundred Jewish tailors worked. There were many affluent people. This is evident from the splendid new synagogue, which is as fine as the one in Petrograd, as well as the other Jewish communal institutions. In the city there were more than forty thousand residents, among them seventeen thousand to eighteen thousand Jews. After the occupation of Lvov, a flood of refugees came here from Lvov and the surrounding shtetls. Before the Russians got here, a large part of the Jewish population, all those with the least bit of money, abandoned everything to the mercy of fate, and fled to Cracow or Vienna. Now hardly five thousand Jews are gathered here, and most of them are refugees from Tuchów, Pilzno, Dębica, and other places. Initially, the Russians took thirty hostages, equal numbers of Poles and Jews. They were detained for several days. A few Poles were then released because the Russians became "convinced of their loyalty." Within twenty-four hours, they let the Jews go too.

They took hostages again yesterday (this time only Jews) and sent them to Pilzno. I was told that a secret order is behind this, driven by the notion that if the Russians leave, the Jews might denounce those Poles who supported the Russians to the Austrian authorities. And now they are taking hostages, and if the Jews happen to issue a denunciation of that kind, then two hostages will be executed for every Pole whom the Austrians kill.

It's simply hard to believe.

Jewish shops that were abandoned by their owners are open for business, and all types of poor educated people (almost always non-Jews) were hired to work there as merchants and given wages. Lord knows what kinds of accounts they keep.

Abandoned apartments have been occupied by the public organizations' military divisions. I saw several of these apartments, all of them Jewish. In nearly every one of them there is a portrait of Herzl on the wall and a Brockhaus encyclopedic dictionary. The interiors in those apartments that are occupied by the public organizations hadn't been touched. The owners' living presence grips your heart. There are postcards on the wall, children's workbooks. But what will become of these apartments and the ones that are now occupied by soldiers and medical orderlies when the current inhabitants leave?

The first people to enter the city were Circassians and they subjected the town to looting. But no one was killed. But then during heavy artillery fire, nearly twenty people were killed in the city. In a spot where a bomb landed, a father and daughter were killed, and the mother and an eleven-year-old boy went mad. A three-year-old child remains.

I ran into Dr. Shabad, who had departed from Petrograd at the same time as me. He was here with the Union of Zemstvos, but there was no work for him and he is going back. He introduced me to a local doctor, Ader, who seems to be the only cultured person left here. There are two Jewish female doctors working for the Union of Zemstvos, Shapiro and Volfson, acquaintances of mine from Switzerland.

Late at night, we heard gunfire from the direction of the front—rapid, continuous, like a drum roll, from rifles and machine guns. It made a terrifying impression on Ratner and me. It was undoubtedly a battle. About four or five versts[114] from us, two rockets suddenly appeared on the far side of a hill, burned out into bright stars, illuminated everything around them, and rapidly faded—an infernal hell. People stab one another, the dead and wounded fall, and everything is covered in blood. And the rattling of gunfire continues. It lasted for two hours.

FEBRUARY 1

I found out that the shooting yesterday was a typical disturbance. There was no fighting whatsoever. Something upset the Austrians and they began to shoot, but not a single person was wounded.

≈

Ratner is taking a trip to Tuchów. Because of my cold I can't go along.

I met Dr. Ader. He described the poverty here. The town council helps the wives of reservists, but only those who, in addition to religious marriages, were also registered at the mayor's office, and there are not many like this among Jews. In general, there are as many as three hundred of these wives, but the total number of those who need aid, or rather are starving and freezing, is not less than 1,500 to 2,000. The rest somehow make ends meet; a number of people are even making a good business of it.

Dr. Gilman stopped by to see me. He has traveled throughout all of Galicia with his division from Lvov and this is what he saw:

Rava-Ruska.[115] Troops arrived there on the 31st.[116] For five days they wrecked the town, and also burned it. Sometimes the officers defended the residents, but most pretended as if they didn't see. This was one scene: soldiers are tearing apart a trading stall. An officer passes by, flings himself at them: "What are you doing, so-and-so?"

"Your Honor,[117] it belongs to yids."

"Ah, yids . . ."

And he walks past.

Huge stocks of eggs have been wrecked; the center of the city was burned. Jews were humiliated, forced to clean barracks. This was often done for a ransom. There were rapes. Dr. Gilman saw a soldier strike down an old man and beat him, and [he] placed the soldier under arrest. He walked on, saw three soldiers bolt from a building, and a Jewish doctor, Gershengorn, run after them, pale as death, holding a revolver in his hand after having caught them raping two girls. One of them was punished with lashings.

Mosti-Velki. Beatings of Jews, the troops looted for five or six days, Ruthenians made off with the spoils.

Niemirów. The whole shtetl was burned.

In Krystynopol and Żydaczów, the troops put horses in synagogues.

Krakowiec. The shtetl was looted, but not burned. Orders were given to open the trading stalls and then soldiers started stealing. The soldiers lit a bonfire on the floor of a house, a fire broke out, and several buildings burned.

Lubaczów. The center of the town is completely burned, not a single shop remains.

Cieszanów. Was turned into a hellhole. Cossacks were there for five days; they raped women, wanted to rape a fifty-eight-year-old woman. They systematically abused people.

In the doctor's opinion, West Galicia suffered less than the East. Jarosław, Łańcut, Żydaczów were looted but not burned. Pilzno, Pińczów too. Dębica is burned. There isn't a single inhabitant left.

In Dr. Gilman's presence, a Pole named Jasinski recounted the following nightmarish fact that occurred in Brzostek. It seems a Jew offended a Cossack in some way. A whole gang of them showed up, grabbed the offender (an old man, along with his son), and led them away to be hanged. They proposed to the son that if he hanged his father they would spare his life. He agreed and hanged his father. Then as they all laughed they hanged him too . . .

Among Ruthenians there is a custom to kiss the hands of estate owners and Jews. And when the Cossacks came to a Jewish estate, they ordered the Ruthenians to expose their backsides and forced the Jews to kiss them.

In Głogów, Cossacks wanted to rape two girls. Their parents stepped in to defend them and all four were killed.

≈

I read announcements in the newspaper from the High Command about the situation in eastern Prussia. It's very depressing. A total retreat. I spoke about the subject with Igor Platonovich. He just returned from High Command headquarters. Radko-Dmitriev is there,[118] says the atmosphere is very joyful, spirits are high, there is faith in victory. At night, we spoke at length about whether there can be rebirth from blood and the horrors of killing. Igor Platonovich claims it is possible. In a time of war, one is forced to kill because of the circumstances, but the general background is suffering and loss, which can regenerate.

I can't agree with him. We argued for a long time. When I asked him if he considers war to be a necessary attribute of human progress, he responded ambivalently. And suddenly he raised the question: "How can you prove that murder is evil?"

Our argument came to an end with that.

≈

I've encountered many officers who have fought in battle or were headed for battle. All of them are peaceful, intensely humble, reluctant to speak about their heroic feats. Your heart is truly moved when you see them. And a thought unwillingly occurs: these people were reborn; they have changed. But your heart can't be reconciled with this notion, that war—killing—can ennoble, regenerate a person. And a savage, horrible thought occurred to me. A person inherits a lust for blood, as he does sexual lust, from distant generations. He doesn't satisfy the passion for blood, and for this reason, a kind of subconscious anxiety exists in every person. And those who do satisfy this lust at war acquire some sort of special tranquility. Everyone in the army possesses some sort of special tranquility. Can there really be a measure of truth in this horror?

FEBRUARY 2

Visited the old synagogue, looked around. It is very beautiful, interesting. A Jew showed me around and poured out his woes. About what. That the army seized the bathhouse and the Hasids can't take a dip in the *mikvah*[119] before prayers.

He showed me a different synagogue, a Hasidic one, which was securely boarded up after it was looted. As a gift, they gave me fragments from ripped Torah scrolls that they bought from a soldier passing through. I went to the New Synagogue. It is very lavish and beautiful, though in a Moorish style. The foundation was laid fifty years ago. But it was completed just last year. People thought it was cursed because some general, a non-Jew, laid the first stone. I found a coppersmith who casts chandeliers in the old ways. In Russia, this industry has vanished. He is incredibly old. He casts modern styles using old-fashioned methods. I bought one candelabrum from him.

FIGURE 1.7. New Jubilee Synagogue, Tarnów. Construction on the synagogue was completed in 1908. William A. Rosenthall Judaica Collection. *Courtesy of College of Charleston Special Collections.*

FEBRUARY 3

I went to the cemetery. People showed me the fresh graves of Jewish soldiers from the Russian Army and the tomb of some local *tsadik*, Reb Shmelke.

Along the way back, they told me that Austrian troops also looted Jewish shops at the time of mobilization.

Ratner returned from Tuchów yesterday. He said the shtetl was completely burned and devastated. The synagogue was turned into a horse stable. Ratner left today to go back to Moscow.

FEBRUARY 5

Yesterday I stayed inside all day with a cold. An old man showed up to see me. He started to tell me that he too is descended from Rapoports,[120] brought quotes from the Bible, and offered verbose explanations about them. In short, a typical schnorrer. But of course that doesn't keep him from starving, and I gave him three rubles. I extricated myself from him with difficulty.

While he was sitting with me, we could hear heavy artillery fire. And all of sudden, there was a screech in the midst of it—sharp, hissing, sinister, and fierce, and in its wake, a powerful boom that made the walls shudder. There was another one just like it twenty minutes later. I went outside and learned that the first bomb landed near the Forty-Second Division Hospital and killed four or five soldiers and ten horses and wounded ten soldiers in a transport. The second bomb landed right near the building where the State Duma Hospital is located. It was a horrible sight. The windows were shattered in each of the surrounding buildings. There is a huge crater behind one building; a crowd is already standing there, and children are looking through shards. In the courtyard in front of the State Duma Hospital, there is a hind part of a horse that was blasted off in the explosion and flung over the roof of a three-story building. There are intestines hanging from trees, pieces of flesh all over the place. They say a soldier was blown apart too. They found a cap and part of a coat with a notebook. But no body parts.

At night, heavy artillery arrived and was placed in the courtyard behind the State Duma Hospital. In the morning, airplanes flew overhead, and at 12:00 o'clock, they fired shots directed at the artillery. Had they fallen five *sazhen*[121] closer, they would have struck the boxes with heavy artillery, and half the city would have gone up in smoke.

The staff at the State Duma Hospital is amazingly calm. They talk of espionage, say people in the city are signaling to the Austrians; there are rumors of an underground telegraph.

※

Dr. Maria L. Shapiro came to see me. She is a doctor with the Union of Towns, a very sensible and nice person. She described how during the first days of mobilization, Poles in Łódź posted up proclamations inciting people to rebel and go over to the Austrian side. At night, Police Chief Geier drove around the city with soldiers and tore them down. She saw and read the proclamations herself.

In Kielce, the Sokóls[122] are spreading agitation.

She was initially stationed with a division in Rava-Ruska. One time the commandant, who was very fond of her, went on at length to her about Jewish dominance, pointed out in passing that the doctor in Rava was a Jew, and suggested she take his place. He was extremely embarrassed when she told him that she is a Jew. She saw dozens of Ruthenians who had been hanged along the road; Magyars who suspected the Ruthenians of treason were responsible for this.

FEBRUARY 6

At night I. P. Demidov came to see me. He thought it necessary to state his credo about the Jewish Question. He is a Judeophile. In his native Tambov province there are no Jews, but the Jews he has encountered in his time were among the finest of people (Harkavy[123] and others). In the Jews, he sees a God-fearing people. But then his attitude wavered a bit. Of course, he knows how many legends and libels there are. In Brody, they said a Jewish girl shot at soldiers. But he heard this legend about the shooting Jewish girl in several other cities—anywhere the city had just been destroyed—and this gives adequate proof that nowhere did any girl shoot anyone. It is equally evident why they always shoot from buildings where there are good stores—stores that are worth looting. He has learned that different standards apply to the Jews: the Russians aren't accustomed to Jewish landownership, nor to hand kissing. And he is very pessimistic about the future. The treatment of the Jews is terrible. Yesterday, there was an explosion, and all at once people began talking about Jewish espionage. He doesn't think the war will bring anything good to the Jews.

"Why have you personally changed your opinion of Jews?"

"It hasn't changed. . . . Of course, there is tactlessness, indiscretion on the part of the Jewish population. They quite candidly express genuine joy over Russian losses. You can get ahold of things only through the Jews, but they take advantage and fleece you. I understand that in general these are trifles, but they are striking, and repulsive."

After the war, there will be a break in life. One must proceed tactfully in raising the Jewish Question. It shouldn't be promoted so intensely at the moment. One has to account for the intelligentsia's psychology, let them resolve the all-Russian, national-Russian question. Otherwise you may become a nuisance or alienate yourself. For example, he thinks the newspaper *Speech*[124] brings more harm than good to the Jews because it overemphasizes the Jewish Question.

FEBRUARY 7

The new commandant had dinner with us today. He spoke of the need for smallpox vaccinations, that ten thousand people urgently need them. There is a great deal he could do in the city, but there are no means for it.

An unexpected opportunity arose to go to Tuchów.[125] I went with Lev Borisovich Trakhtman, a doctor from the State Duma's First Flying Column,[126] and Baron Tsenker.

The road was very scenic, mountains and hills that gently transition to valleys. There is greenery everywhere. The weather is almost spring-like. Here and there, peasants are tilling. Along the road there are several manors and villages; some of the buildings were destroyed, nearly all of them display traces of the soldiers and horses that were stationed there.

On both sides of the road, there are heaps of tin cans, Austrian and ours, rusting cartridge clips with cartridges, broken lanterns, axles, and so forth. In some spots you can see trenches partly caved in or covered over, both Austrian and ours.

We reached the town at eight o'clock, when it was already dark. Both sides of the whole main street that leads to the marketplace were burned; remnants of three-story stone buildings remain; in some buildings, nothing is left apart from chimneys and sunken tin roofs. In the marketplace and beyond, the buildings are intact but empty; not a single one of them has any windowpanes; they have nothing but bare walls and straw on the floor. Heads of horses are sticking out from the windows of one-story houses. The synagogue is big and new; it was built eleven years ago. It wasn't burned, but the windows are broken, the doors are wide open, and inside all that remains is an ark with gilding. Everything else was decimated. There is no pulpit, no platform, no benches, no lights, no scrolls—nothing. The walls are bare. There are scraps of religious books and chandelier fragments lying scattered about on the floor mixed up with straw. The corners of the room and adjoining chapels were fouled, not by horses, but by people. They turned a temple into a latrine.

I met with the hospital detachment that is run by Igor Platonovich's wife, Ekaterina Iurievna. She is a very cultured, educated, joyful, energetic,

FIGURE 1.8. Husakov, a shtetl in Galicia (now Ukraine), 1915. Bernard Bardach Collection. *Courtesy of the Leo Baeck Institute, New York.*

glowing woman, not at all suitable for a mystic. But she's an occultist, a theosophist. She spoke of military parades, the awarding of crosses, how beautiful all of it was. It seems the external appearance of things impresses her a great deal.

There was a Colonel Nechvolodov[127] here from the Baturin Regiment. He looks like an eccentric, enunciates his words somehow fancifully and speaks in such a way that you don't know if he is joking or serious, reminds you of the sort of actor who really puts on airs. They say he's a senselessly brave man. He walked eight hundred paces in advance of his regiment during a battle, has earned every distinction, captured some city, or won a major victory. In general, the Baturin Regiment is renowned.

He invited us to visit the regiment tomorrow, which is stationed in reserves on an estate, near the front, to see the show their company is staging. He invited me too.

FEBRUARY 8

I walked around the town. Its appearance doesn't lend itself to description. The few buildings that remain have been fouled. The streets are filled with impassable mud. There isn't a single trading stall. Hardly any inhabitants can be spotted. There are still Christians here and there, but no Jews. . . . But here comes an old man with *peyes* and a long caftan, carrying a tallis[128] under his arm. He walked up the mud-filled street, to a spot where there were stones on the ground, stepped on one, gathered his coat flaps, spent a long time preparing to take the next step, lost his coat flaps, caught them again, hopped over, and scampered off somewhere. A young man who followed him repeated his moves. I didn't see where they entered. And again the Jews were gone. I walked to the town square. There were soldiers in the town hall; boxes with munitions and horses in the square. Empty counters in the trading stalls. Empty buildings; near some shops, there are bundles of mud-covered hay here and there.

I saw soldiers leaving one house, others going in, and asked them where to buy cigarettes. They pointed to that building. An old Jew and a boy live there. It was packed with soldiers who were buying various things. I asked for cigarettes. They'd sold their last ones and directed me to another house. I went there. It too was filled with soldiers. An old man was selling cigarettes, honey cakes, and chocolate. A young man wearing tefillin[129] was standing in the corner and praying; an old, despondent woman was sitting in a chair; a young woman was helping the old man. There were two girls loafing around the house. A handicapped man with a stiff hand and a paralyzed leg was sitting to the side. I bought cigarettes, waited for the customers to thin out, and started chatting with the old man. The little town used to be prosperous and attractive. There were one hundred Jewish families; now there are twenty poor, sick, old people left, the rest ran away.

The Russians arrived three weeks after Sukkot.[130] They looted all the shops, but the town was left intact. The Russians stayed for four weeks and then withdrew. The Austrians came and were here for a week. Then the Russians started bombing and utterly wrecked the town. Buildings burned at the time. After that, the Russians returned and have now been here for eight weeks. During the bombing, the population fled a distance of ten kilometers from the town.

We began to talk about the synagogue. They hid the Torah scrolls behind a makeshift brick wall, but apparently badly—soldiers busted open the wall, found the scrolls, and ripped some of them, but the people managed to get them back. The old woman who had been sitting to the side and silently listening to the story about the pogrom stood up when the Torah scroll was mentioned, walked over, and declared:

"They took the Torah scrolls, they put them under the horses' hooves..."

Her voice shook and she broke down in tears and sobbed. I asked her about it. She is from Dębica. She used to buy and sell product parts. But Dębica was burned. She looked just as she had when she escaped: "I found this shirt I'm wearing here in a pile of rubbish, washed it, and put it on." She has three sons in America. One of them, who is forty-three years old, was drafted into the army, and left behind seven children. She is alone. I gave several rubles to her and to the poor baker who owns the house.

I went there again in the afternoon. I was besieged by a *melamed*[131] and a blind old man who began to complain that the owner of the house didn't give them anything. I gave them each just one crown. An old man approached me too. He was a rich man, and now the baker gave him one crown, the same as what he gave to the poor. This is a real insult.

A tragedy within a tragedy. At five o'clock, Colonel Nechvolodov arrived with three carriages and drove all of us to his show. There was Ekaterina Iurievna Demidova, her sister Sofia Iurievna Novosiltseva, the young countess Bobrinskaia, Dr. Trakhtman, the young count Bobrinskii, Baron Tsenker, and myself.

The regiment is stationed on a large estate just one verst[132] from Tuchów. It is in reserves. They spend two weeks at the front, two in reserves. The trenches run in a parallel line, a quarter of an hour's walk from there. Of course, cannon fire and individual shots could be heard. The Twelfth Regiment has to return to the front. And in these past ten days, they prepared a show.

A huge barn had been completely adorned in willow branches. The whole company sat along the length of the barn. There were seven or eight children of local residents sitting in front and two or three women. All of the regiment's officers were standing near the entrance, twenty men who were introduced to us. They handed us programs that were drawn by hand, with sketches that were quite good for an ordinary artist. They seated us in the first row.

There was a stage, prompter, booth, curtain with a winter landscape: trees in the snow, a peasant hut with a flame in the window.

"If you look closely you can see Pakhom[133] frying potatoes in the hut," someone joked. It was clear that great effort had gone into it.

The program. Three acts. And it had everything: a choir, storytelling, dancing, clowning, singing, and fighting. The star was Khaiutin, who'd been in Kharkov working at a common nightclub and was now a soldier. He recently converted (he's a Jew), and Demidova and one of the officers were the christeners. That's why he's part of this company.

They began with a hymn, of course. Then a choir of twenty men sang. The voices were quite good, especially one baritone. They sang mostly Ukrainian songs, but several in Russian as well. The Ukrainian songs were sentimental and sad; the Russian ones strong and boisterous. They invested an enormous amount of feeling in both. And in both of them you felt the connection between the condition of these twenty tall, strong, young people and the spirit of their singing. There was so much deep, powerful sadness in their situation, and it seemed they were pouring out their woes about all of the terrible hardships, horrors, and misfortunes of the past and the future. And then they switched to happy, fierce Russian songs, and you felt all the bravery and courage and strength of these young men. In general, in this setting, every word was endowed with symbolism and had its own special significance. You can hear the phrase "death to our enemies" so many times, and it makes no impression on you whatsoever. But here you immediately feel the whole terrible, real meaning of these words on the lips of people who only yesterday went into hand-to-hand combat with the enemy and will do it again tomorrow. And there was just as real, dreadfully real significance, in the words "our comrades who died in battle, you are our crown of thorns." They sang so conscientiously and earnestly!

The clowning was suited to the soldiers' tastes. There were jokes of this sort: "I'm a photographer." "What do you take?" "Coats, watches, rings and anything else for the taking." They told riddles. Some of them got laughs.

"Why is a piglet the most wretched of all creatures?"

"All he has is his mother, and she's a pig."

"Why did God create the potato?"

"The rich skin the poor, the poor skin the potatoes."

Khaiutin recited several poems very well and performed scenes from Ukrainian everyday life even better. Of course, that convert couldn't restrain himself from making jokes at the expense of Jews. One little soldier performed a Russian folk dance nicely. A battalion commander in full battle dress was standing next to me the whole time. His battalion was on active duty and he could have been called up at any moment. At the high point of the show an orderly came and reported to him: "There is no fighting, everything is quiet."

"Excellent," the colonel replied. During the intermission he chatted with the officers. They spoke about soldiers and their psychology.

> What is especially invaluable is their confidence in victory. Soldiers will be sitting in the trenches, having a meal. All of a sudden there is a command: "Attack!" And I myself have witnessed such a scene: a soldier stuffs his last bits of kasha into his pockets, sticks straw onto a bayonet, and runs. He doesn't doubt for a second that he'll capture their trenches, and he moves there with all of his possessions, his supper and bed.
>
> It's hard for a soldier to pick himself up when he's lying in the trenches. But once he gets up and gets moving he goes without frustration. You won't find a child who is more obedient. He waits—silence, you can hear them breathing, you whisper an order, and everyone hears it.
>
> Of course, there are stragglers who hide behind peasant huts, but no more than two percent are like that. Sometimes you glance at them and cross yourself. Thank God you have so few good-for-nothings in your company. Those are the types who go missing. Most of the time they get wounded, since there are more bullets the farther back you are. As you walk toward a battle you can't recall a thing. You're too nervous. Once everything is over you come back to your senses, and at that point some sort of terrible thirst for action surfaces in you. You form lines and give orders to clear the wounded.

After the show, the colonel walked on to the stage, and the actors' voices echoed from behind the curtain: "Glad to serve, Your Excellency!"

The officers liked the show. Afterward there was a lavish dinner with wine, cognac, even ice cream. There were toasts and salutations. On behalf of the guests, Trakhtman made a toast to the estate's owner and the colonel. As someone visiting from Russia, I said several words about the mood in Russia and conveyed greetings from the motherland and solemn reverence for their feats. The colonel replied that the awareness that Russia is behind them gives them courage and strength.

It was very intimate and heartfelt. We left late, accompanied by cheers and good wishes. They wanted to send us off with shots and fireworks, but the colonel forbade it, fearing it would raise an alarm.

FEBRUARY 9

I left for Tarnów. A fatigued soldier from the Baturin Regiment drove me. Along the way he said this: "During the Japanese campaign, the officers were reprimanded for taking cover while the soldiers went under fire. But now, here, seeing the officers makes you want to cry, believe me. They're the first ones to crawl under fire. They live with the soldiers in the trenches for months at a time. But you see, they aren't accustomed to it, it's harder for them. They bear so much grief! Really. And during battles you have to restrain them with force, hide them behind yourself. They'll get killed and the chain will be left without command."

It seems Igor Platonovich left for two days. Prior to his departure, he told me that P. D. Dolgorukov,[134] who arrived five days ago, had taken an interest in my offer to travel around Galicia to look for shoe leather, and would like to speak with me. I saw him and he asked me to meet the day after tomorrow in the morning.

≈

There are announcements posted up around the city in Polish and German about Jewish hostility toward the Russian Army in Galicia and Poland, and the taking of Jewish hostages in case Jews denounce Poles to the Austrians. The poster also says that there should be no Jews left west of Jarosław. And all of this is confirmed by the opinion of the High Command. There are no signatures on the posters.

The poster made an extremely painful impression on the Jewish population. They see this as a plain attempt to incite the Polish population against the Jews.

FIGURE 1.9. Jewish bread peddler in Tarnów. Photograph taken during World War I. *Courtesy of the YIVO Institute for Jewish Research, New York.*

≈

Dr. Ader came to see me. He spoke about the poster, said it would be worthwhile to bring it to the attention of the High Command. Jews, he says, consider the accusation of espionage to be a supreme insult. They are peaceful, loyal residents and don't get mixed up in politics. There isn't a single fact that proves Jews are engaged in spying. Yet Jews are taken from the streets for hard labor; they're nabbed on the streets, fifty people at once, men and women. There is one *melamed* here who goes around extorting money, threatening to denounce someone if they are able to go out to work.

≈

I ran into Prince Dolgorukov. He asked me to visit him the day after tomorrow to discuss my mission.

FEBRUARY 11

Yesterday I spent the whole day writing. Today I went to see the Prince, but he postponed our conversation again until tomorrow because he's going to Tuchów.

≈

I went to get a haircut. The barber naively described how remarkable the Jews in this town used to be—lawyers, doctors. What great orators they were. During a mayoral election, one of them gave a speech and declared he would speak as a Jew and a Zionist. The antisemites didn't want to give him the floor, but he forced them to hear him out.

The most sinister rumors are coming from eastern Prussia. Our corps was annihilated or taken prisoner. Another is imperiled.

FEBRUARY 12

I spoke with P. D. Dolgorukov. He finds that I could perform a great service if I traveled around to look for leather and shoes. I agreed. I went to the headquarters of the Ninth Corps to gather information about standard values, but they told me I could find out about this at the Central Administration in Lvov or Kiev.

≈

Igor Platonovich arrived. He says he just heard news from eastern Prussia. Our side beat back forty-two attacks. The corps didn't fall, but rather, is in the forests. Germans are bypassing them on either side. He suggested that I take a managerial post in Lvov, in addition to my travels for leather. We'll see. We'll talk about it tomorrow.

FEBRUARY 13

The announcements from High Command about the retreat from eastern Prussia are terrible.[135] It's clear that nearly the whole corps is dead.

Dr. Raisa Iakovna Volfson from the Union of Towns is going to Dąbrowa, eighteen versts[136] from here, where a meal station is being opened. She has been there, said the shtetl is burned, destroyed. The population is starving. She saw fifty Jews being forced to clean the streets. There were youth too, practically children. She promised photographs. I gave her several rubles for the poor.

I received traveling documents from the Union of Towns and the State Duma that designate me as a plenipotentiary. I can leave. There are no wagons available right now. The first half of my task is finished.

FEBRUARY 13, TARNÓW

I was entirely set to leave when something shocking and unexpected occurred. I was sitting with Demidov and discussing plans for our trip, when all of a sudden there was a deafening boom from an explosion, as if a multiple-story building had collapsed. The windowpanes shattered into smithereens. We immediately realized a bomb landed, and somewhere very close by. My first thought: we survived. And a torrent of shouting: "The devil take it, another one!" We ran from the house pale and intensely solemn, and saw that a bomb fell in a spot at a distance of about thirty to forty *sazhen*,[137] where it hit and demolished Dr. Ader's house. I won't describe my impressions or the destruction that resulted from the bomb in detail; I'll write about it in correspondence. I will only say that this explosion, and a second one that followed an hour later, which smashed a huge Gymnasium building where an officer's club was stationed in half, did not produce the sort of panic one might have expected. In the second instance, there were no casualties. In the first, a woman and child in a tailor's house were killed. Ader miraculously survived because he left his house a half an hour before the explosion. A woman and a young man, an apprentice, were wounded. The woman lost her leg and hand; the apprentice had a broken back. I saw him in the hospital; he was in a feverish state, and began speaking to me. A few hours later he was dead. And the woman died at night. The street is in shambles; you can hear wailing.

And there are once again whispers and insinuations of signals and espionage among the army and hospital workers. A bomb hit Dr. Ader's house because the Automobile Company is stationed nearby, and the Gymnasium, because the officer's club is there.

I was calm during the bombing, but in the evening and late at night, I was in a nervous state. It seemed that at any moment there would be an echo of a deafening boom and a bomb would hit the hotel.

At night I went to the bank and spoke with Prince Dolgorukov. The commandant, Markevich, was there too. He was very worried, assured us that High Command was recouping. When he found out I was leaving he requested permission to visit me tomorrow morning.

Correspondence.

FEBRUARY 14

Markevich came to see me in the morning. The purpose of his visit was to ask that I deliver a letter and greeting to his wife in Kiev. We spoke about the bombing, of course. He was very concerned and spent the whole time pointing out that it was senseless to bomb a city that had no military presence.

"I think it's necessary to somehow inform them of this," he said.

"Who?"

"The Austrians."

"And will they believe you?"

"Not me. I have it in mind to speak with the mayor and bishop, so that they write a letter to the Austrians saying they are bombing a city where there is nothing but hospitals and a peaceful population, and somehow deliver this letter through High Command."

This seemed odd to me, but I didn't say anything. Then he told me about the speech he drafted to give to the city's leaders. He recognizes that the city's inhabitants haven't yet become Russian subjects and he isn't demanding their support, merely their loyalty; that they refrain from getting mixed up in politics. He stated that his main wish was for his speech to be published somewhere and offered to give me the text. We drove to his apartment.

As we were approaching his building and stopping, a gentleman rode past on a horse-drawn wagon. He too stopped, walked over to Markevich, greeted him. Markevich introduced me to him, saying this was the mayor, and for several minutes they spoke in Polish. Markevich spoke obsequiously, but the gentleman was cold. From the conversation, I vaguely grasped that it concerned the bombing of the city and an appeal to Austrian headquarters.

"It seems your conversation was about that letter to the Austrians," I said.

"Yes . . . ," Markevich sourly replied, "he found out about it, and here he says to me, 'I don't know about the bishop, but I won't write such a letter. You can hang me, of course, but I won't do it.' 'Why not?' I asked him. 'Because if I were to send such a letter, a bomb would hit the town hall within an hour.' 'And without that letter it can't hit the town hall?' 'Without it a bomb can't fall there . . .' There it is. Now I will simply seize and occupy the town hall, and propose to him that he live at headquarters."

On a desk in the chancellery I found two large stacks of the notorious announcements regarding Jewish espionage. I asked Markevich what sort of announcements these were. He looked embarrassed and said he had nothing to do with them. On the contrary, he had sought to avoid posting the announcements for as long as he could. I asked him for several copies of it for the [Jewish] museum, and he allowed me to take as many as I wanted.

I ran into doctors Gilman and M. L. Shapiro. Gilman recounted several impressions. When Russian forces occupied Jarosław, he was there too. The nights were especially terrible. Darkness. Profound silence. Suddenly, from one house, then from another, a woman's desperate, heart-rending scream resounds and is abruptly broken off, as if someone shut the screaming woman's mouth. These were soldiers going around the houses, stealing and raping.

Gilman spent time in Brody; he came there two days after the destruction of the city and categorically affirms that neither an *esaul* nor a Cossack was killed or wounded. He was well acquainted with the whole unit, was stationed with it for a long time, and would have known if something like that had happened. The whole myth of a "Jewish girl shooting from a window" was a typical provocation that was repeated everywhere. In one location (Jarosław it seems), this broke out: shots were fired and soldiers jumped out shouting that yids were shooting from a house. But it turned out that the whole house was occupied exclusively by Russian officers. The soldiers were prosecuted, and some of them even punished. Gilman talked about extortion. In Nowe Miasto, the commandant ordered all the Jews to be taken for labor. They were driven out on to the streets; there were lethal beatings. On the second or third day, he ordered them to clean the latrines and forced the rabbi's assistant to do this. "And tomorrow the rabbi will clean the toilets." When the Jews finally figured it out, they collected 1,800 rubles and gave it to him. That commandant is now gone. He requested a position at the front once while he was drunk. He was sent there. He then tried with all his might to stay where he was, but it didn't help.

≈

I left in the afternoon. I was given a car ride as far as Dębica. There were two nurses riding in the car; one of them was wounded, the other was accompanying her. The latter had a brother, Shtal, stationed at the headquarters in Pilzno. We stopped in Pilzno[138] for a half an hour, drank tea, met the brother. He introduced me to a colonel who was the director of the Division of Intelligence. I told him I was collecting various war-related documents and proclamations for a museum.

"We have a good number of those and can give them to you. Let me ask my superior, Aleksandr Ivanov Zvegintsev."[139]

Zvegintsev arrived and all he wanted to know was the museum for which I was collecting, and without even asking who I am, allowed them to give me the proclamations. They gave me ten different official Austrian proclamations as well as unofficial documents in Russian and in Turkish. They gave me a packet of letters that had been taken from a plane in Przemyśl. The only request they made was that the documents were not to be published. I noted my receipt of them in my own accounts, but they didn't ask me for that either.

I found the notorious "announcement" on a desk and asked where they had gotten it. "High Command headquarters sent us fifty thousand copies of these to post."

"But why aren't there any signatures at the bottom?" I inquired.

"That isn't required."

I walked around the town. It is relatively intact. There were Jews moving about everywhere (Purim begins tonight). I wanted to meet the rabbi but didn't have time. I went to look for the synagogue. It was near a river on a dirty side street—small, decrepit, wooden, neglected. An old Jew led me to it. There were soldiers spread out on the ground occupying the vestibule and women's section. The sanctuary wasn't occupied, but it was empty and had been stripped. When I began talking with the old man, he told me:

"They robbed and hauled off everything. On the pulpit there was a silver *mizrakh*,[140] remarkable work. It was worth 400 crowns—they ripped it off."

I walked out to the other side. There were soldiers sitting down, keeping busy with various tasks. There was an ark behind curtains on the wall and books on the shelves.

"What's going on in here?" I asked the soldiers.

"It's their temple! Let it be. We don't touch it."

We continued driving. I forgot to mention earlier that I had left Tarnów with papers from Prince Dolgorukov and Demidov stating that they were instructing me to find leather for army divisions. We arrived in Dębica right as the transport train was leaving, and I just managed to catch it. It was dark, stuffy, crowded in the train compartment.

I talked with a man from a railroad battalion who was at the rail station in Tarnów during the first bombing on January 1, and he conveyed his impressions:

We celebrated the New Year with a festive, loud party and went to sleep at four or five o'clock. All of a sudden there was a terrifying crash. Without having a clue, I pulled myself together and ran from the room wearing nothing but my undershirt. It was already eleven or twelve o'clock. My first thought was that they dropped a bomb from an airplane. I look up, can't see a thing. I ask the others, they don't know anything either. Well I for one didn't rack my brains over it. I went back to my room and laid down again. Just as I started to doze off there was another crash, an even stronger one. I got dressed and ran outside. It seems the water tower was smashed and one man was badly wounded. We then finally understood they were firing at us with heavy artillery. And we had a whole train filled with weapons at the station, the Empress Maria Fyodorovna. We went to call our superiors at headquarters, and from there they ordered us to immediately remove everything from the station. And so our work went into full swing. And bombs were falling on us every twenty minutes, like clockwork, one after another. And in the course of the day twenty-one bombs were dropped that destroyed eleven out of thirteen rail lines, badly damaged the Maria Fyodorovna, killed or wounded six to eight people, and maimed ten horses. However, we managed to remove everything, and most importantly the weapons.

It was awful. Especially after twenty minutes went by, and you would wait—any second now it'll explode. We hid behind the train cars. I saved myself by quickly propping up a barricade during the explosions. One time the impact of a bomb threw me to the ground and dragged me several *sazhen* through the mud. The most sensible thing to do was to hit the ground. But somehow it didn't enter your mind to throw yourself willingly into mud. When I finished working that night, I drove off and arrived in a place twenty versts[141] away, and my hands and legs were trembling. And suddenly a new order was issued—leave for the station and bring something back from there. It took a huge amount of willpower to force myself to go. It was dark there when I approached. And my feet wouldn't have moved even if you had dragged them.

In the train car, there was a young man wearing doctor's insignia. His speech was semiliterate and rude, and it was strange to imagine him as a doctor. I questioned him, and he replied he was a military doctor. We began talking about his impressions of military life, and he went on and on about his daring exploits.

"I was real good at settling scores with yids. With them nothing got through except the whip and stick I used to flog them."

"For what?"

"For everything! They're filthy scum. I don't treat them like people, but like dogs."

"Why is that?"

"They always hid their supplies. 'Have nothing,' they'd say. But give 'em a taste of the whip and they find it all."

There were other doctors in the train car that glanced over. They shrugged their shoulders. Later when we had gone out to a platform, one of them said to me: "What a swine, that military doctor! It's shameful to listen to him. Why, I'm certain he's no military doctor, but a feldsher[142] who's training in the lower ranks. I'll bring him out into the open."

FEBRUARY 15

On the platform in Rava-Ruska, a ten year-old Jewish girl was carrying around old newspapers. A gendarme seized the newspapers from her and hauled her off to the commandant.

"Why are you dragging her off? What has she done?"

"They can't hang around, they spy here."

This is a ten-year-old girl some three hundred versts from the front. Pure insanity.

≈

The doctor and students pressed the so-called military doctor.

"In which university did you study?"

"In Kazan."

"Name a professor who lectured there."

He got confused and named a professor who lectures in Kiev. Everyone burst out laughing—and he wilted. As we approached Lvov, the "military doctor" began to say goodbye and extended his hand to me.

"I won't shake your hand," I said. "I don't shake hands with charlatans, or the likes of you!"

He shrank and scampered off like a beaten dog.

Lvov.

On the request of P. D. Dolgorukov, I stopped by the Union of Towns Committee, where a plenipotentiary had borrowed a car from Dolgorukov for several days and, despite his telegrams, had not returned it. The plenipotentiary, Iona Brekhnichev, informed me with the naivety of a child that he crashed the car and has no time to get it fixed. Then he began complaining to me about everyone and everything that insults him. He struck me as an immature man with a swollen sense of pride. And the main supervision of Union of Towns divisions for the Southwestern Front is in the hands of a man like this.

I met with Dr. Hausner. He hadn't yet been to see Bobrinskii. In light of the numerous misfortunes that have befallen the Russian Army, Bobrinskii is not in a very benevolent mood. And in general, his situation is indeed rather difficult. He is between three fires. From one side the Muscophiles, with Evlogii and Dulkevich among them, are promoting Russification policies; from another side there is the pressure of the Polish nobility. From a third side, there is the influence of the military sphere. Apart from that, there are purely military policies issued by High Command. And all of these currents agree on one thing alone: a tendency to put pressure on Jews. Bobrinskii, on his part, would like to administer decent policies. He doesn't believe in "Jewish espionage," and at the very least, would like to be fair in his approach to the

FIGURE 1.10. Hasidic synagogue on Boznicza Street, Lvov, after a fire, 1915. *Courtesy of the Center for Urban History of East Central Europe, L'viv.*

Jews. But he is powerless. As for allowing plenipotentiaries to travel to distribute aid to Jews in Galicia, this lies beyond his purview.

The Tarnów announcement about Jewish espionage made the most depressing, almost shocking impression on Hausner. He thinks this heralds the destruction of Galician Jewry. Among prominent people there are nine thousand Jews who can be seized in three hundred locations that are occupied by the Russians. He begged me to not lose a second—to leave for Petrograd and rouse the Jewish leadership there to adopt some sort of measures to save Galician Jewry. This is incomparably more important than any kind of monetary aid.

He told me that a priest came by and told one of his acquaintances that he (Hausner) should try to go into hiding, because he (the priest) was certain that Hausner would be arrested, if not today, then tomorrow, and that a decidedly sad fate was in store for him. Hausner replied that he refused to hide. When he chose to stay in Lvov, he knew what he was in for and that he was risking his life. But his duties compelled him to stay, and he is staying until the end. He asked me to petition Deputy Fridman to come to Lvov.

FEBRUARY 16

I left for Kiev.

FEBRUARY 17, KIEV

A rumor is going around that Bobrinskii is leaving. Trepov[143] is supposed to be appointed in his place, but he is dying, and Kurlov[144] will be appointed.

A committee[145] meeting was held. Bykhovskii reported on his meeting with the commander of the Kiev military district, concerning the issue of expellees from Galicia; the latter made a rather vague promise. The Tarnów "announcement" made an abysmal impression here too. We talked about Margolin's[146] trip to see General Ivanov at headquarters, but don't expect that anything will come of it.

FEBRUARY 18

I left for Petrograd. During the trip, I met an officer who said many interesting things. A hospital train carrying the wounded passed us, most of them hand wounds. The officer glanced through the window and casually noted, "self-inflicted."

"What does that mean?"

"It means they wounded themselves. Ninety-five out of one hundred are like that—wounded in the hand. Now they get short shrift. If someone comes in with a shot-off finger, they'll bandage him, give him twenty-five lashes, and send him back to the trenches without further discussion. As soon as we began to do that the hand wounds stopped. . . . With my division here it was the same story. . . . They poke their arms out from the trenches and wait for a bullet to catch them. I saw this happen and punished them. A day or two goes by, I go over to the trench, and the soldiers are lying down, lifting their legs and jerking them around: "Maybe they'll shoot my leg! Ha ha!" But you know, I don't judge them either. I was wounded in my hipbone here. One millimeter deeper and kaput. But I was lucky. And here I was able to rest for a month and a half in a warm place, see my family, come back to my senses. And now I'm going back. But everyone wants even just a little break. Otherwise it's very hard. People are exhausted. Believe me, I had to use a stick, a whip, and sometimes even a revolver to force people into combat. And if they made it to the position I had to threaten them again with a stick to force them to dig in. 'Dig in . . . look—they'll kill you!' And he: 'Oh, it doesn't matter, Your Excellency, let them kill me, I don't have the strength to go on!' There were times you might be in combat for two or three days without eating or drinking anything. After something like that you become wooden, you feel nothing, react to nothing. You begin to eat but can't taste anything. It's especially terrible if you experience a sudden panic attack. Sometimes it flares up for no reason, especially in the darkness, at night. We were stationed in a village. I don't know what happened, but suddenly there was shouting: 'They're surrounding us!' Shots were fired. People started to flee: 'Retreat, retreat!' And I got carried away. Fortunately, a colonel jumped out: 'Where are you—turn around or I'll shoot!' We came to our senses and turned around. In general, nighttime panic attacks are not uncommon among us. They are now even mentioned in our textbooks."

Three or four unionists[147] from Kiev have been sitting in the restaurant car all day. They are shady characters from the looks of them: clever, garrulous, sarcastic, and semiliterate. I saw one of them at the Beilis Trial,[148] hanging around Shmakov's[149] and Zamyslovskii's[150] tails the whole time. Now they are sitting, gossiping, talking about some kind of business deals. Now and then they bring up politics. A phrase reaches me: "We ought to expel the Jews—and there will be no spies."

Another states: "A German plane was shot down, landed on our position, and there in the plane were two Jews from the next town over."

They are also talking about some unionist paper.

FEBRUARY 19, PETROGRAD

I went to see F. K. Sologub. He was terribly distraught over what is happening in Galicia, was regretting having written poems for the Poles.

A. N. Chebotarevskaia[151] whispered to me: "F. K. is now quite distant from his formerly militant spirit; his poems express different themes now, social ones."

I saw Pozner and he told me that a league for the defense of Jewish rights[152] was established here. Gorky, Andreev, and Sologub are running it. They have involved every relatively prominent writer and academic. They composed a declaration with hundreds of signatures, sent around a questionnaire in order to conduct a survey about the Jewish Question. They are planning to publish anthologies.

FEBRUARY 20

There was a committee meeting today for the Political Bureau,[153] to which I relayed my observations and presented a copy of the Tarnów announcement about Jewish espionage and hostages. It made a terrible impression on everyone. The following resolutions were adopted: 1) to take this document to the Chairman of the Council of Ministers[154] and draw his attention to it; 2) to talk it over with the English diplomat, Buchanan;[155] 3) to circulate a copy of this document; 4) to write a report about it to High Command; 5) to insist that D. S. Margolin go to headquarters to discuss the announcement with General Ivanov.

FEBRUARY 21

Perelman[156] came to see me. He said that a Jewish newspaper is being organized in Petrograd and proposed that I join its editorial board. I declined, not only for the technical reason that I can't be in Petrograd, but also because I don't believe anything will come of it. Perelman is always fussing over plans from which nothing materializes.

I saw Pozner. He is insisting that I draw up a calendar for the *Almanac* by the first of April. Otherwise . . . otherwise they will assign the task of compiling it to someone else. The same comedy is repeated every year. They hurry up and then publish it around November.

I saw Miliukov,[157] gave him a copy of the Tarnów announcement, and described for him in detail what is going on in Galicia. He promised on his part to meet with Sazonov[158] about this matter. He asked that I provide him with detailed information. In general, he's rather restrained when it comes to the Jewish Question.

Leaving for Moscow.

FEBRUARY 22

Naidich informed me that in Moscow he collected 30,000 rubles for Palestinian Jews. The Moscow Committee allotted me 1,000 rubles to aid Galician Jews.

I went to see L. P. Demidov. He was complaining that the funds of the State Duma Hospital's Moscow division are drying up. I wrote to Pozner with a request that he obtain some money for the division in Petrograd.

FEBRUARY 24

On my way to Lvov. During the trip I met an officer on crutches. He was in a relentless mood. He says we shouldn't take prisoners, but rather we should run all of them through. We must annihilate Germany. A doctor who was also riding in the car, Sekretarev, was arguing with him. The officer said that in Tarnopol one priest and three Jews were hanged for spying, and that all of them should be hanged. The Germans act atrociously and we too should be atrocious. There should be no mercy for civilians. We have to terrorize them. One time, the Germans were shooting and struck a water tower with precision. That means they were directing the gunfire. The doctor retorted in an original manner: "As for me," he said, "none of my spiritual riches are my own. All that I have comes from the Germans and Jews. I studied in Germany and we take everything from them. We, like the Russians, have nothing of our own. We are slaves of Germany. And we ought to liberate ourselves from them, to create our own, and not to annihilate Germany."

FEBRUARY 25, KIEV

The Relief Committee gave me 8,000 rubles for my proposal to travel around the larger locations in occupied Galicia to investigate the situation of Jews there and give them a sum of money for Passover. D. S. Margolin promised to go see General Ivanov at headquarters.

The Society for the Defense of Women is sending two members to Galicia to construct a girls' shelter and become generally familiar with the problem of prostitution and the struggle against it. They suggested that one Jew travel with this group. They chose Goldenveizer,[159] the assistant barrister and son of the famous lawyer. He was asking me about Galicia. I gave him whatever information I could. There is apparently one lady, Golubkova, who is going with him. I don't believe they'll manage to do anything substantial. But it can't hurt them to go and see what is happening there with their own eyes. At least they can gather information about hundreds of raped girls.

I visited the quartermaster to obtain shoe patterns, since I'll be traveling throughout Galicia and searching for leather and shoes. One of the clerks was looking me over somehow very attentively, and asked in a whisper: "Isn't the situation of Jews terrible indeed? They're getting killed and robbed!" He's a Jew, evidently, and is surely hiding his Jewishness. There are so many Marranos about now.

I'm leaving for Lvov.

FEBRUARY 26

During the trip, I met Dr. Epshtein, who said many wild things about the Wild Division, under the command of Grand Duke Mikhail Aleksandrovich.[160]

Lvov. I went to see Hausner. I relayed everything I accomplished in Petrograd and Kiev in regard to the Tarnów announcement and that I was carrying money for Passover. Of course, he was grateful for this. But there are now new and specific hardships, in addition to the general ones. Jews have lost the right to travel from one district to another. In the miniscule districts here that means a paralysis of trade. But even apart from that, Jews are virtually deprived of the ability to travel from place to place, even within the districts themselves. The rail lines and even the stations are absolutely closed to Jews (not once have I seen a single Jew even near a station) and moving around on wagons is so risky that most won't bring themselves to do it. And now a new order has been issued here that government and military establishments are to cease all commercial relations with Jews, even those from Russia. In general, entry to Galicia is closed to Jews from Russia. All of this has caused terrible inflation and virtually a famine. Hausner went to see Governor Bobrinskii about this matter and reminded him that even Sodom was granted absolution on account of ten righteous people, and here a whole region was being subjected to the horrors of starvation. He recited his whole speech for me, with quotes from the Bible and prophets. He concluded the speech with a citation from Victor Hugo: [illegible].

Bobrinskii promised Hausner to "think about it." Hausner also spoke with Mayor Rutowski,[161] asked that he intervene for the Jews, and reproached him for washing his hands of the matter: "We always served you faithfully and honestly through hell and high water, as Jacob served Laban, and now you abandon us, wretched and helpless," he said. In general, Rutowski is more or less a decent person. In addition, he is uncertain as to whether the Austrians will come back and tries to treat the Jews properly. He promised Hausner he would go to Bobrinskii.

FEBRUARY 27

I traveled to Zholkva to meet with Dr. Lander. I arrived in the city during a snowstorm, but was nonetheless overwhelmingly amazed by the little city's beauty. The whole main square could be placed inside a museum as one piece. Castle ruins, towers, a fortress wall, a remarkable Catholic Church, a statue of Sobiesky.[162] There are many historic and artistic treasures and relics here. A prisoner was being held in the tower. The Żółkiewsky family grave is inside the church.[163] There are also Rubens paintings there. Interestingly, the inscription on the Sobiesky monument was erased because it was written in Polish. These are the bizarre outrages that our Russification of the region has produced.

The town is intact. Trading stalls are open. However, Jews are glancing around fearfully and bowing subserviently. There is a unit of the so-called Wild Ones or Wild Divisions stationed here, about whom much is said. These are Caucasian mountaineers—short, swarthy Asiatics. They ride small, muscular horses with which they seem to be fused, and sport red hoods across their backs. I saw some of them during the day. A division was passing through the marketplace. One of them walked in front playing a *zurna*;[164] others followed him, some performing dances, the rest clapping their hands. All of it was done in a somber, slow rhythm, like a ritual.

I found Lander and got acquainted. He made a very good impression. He is passionately devoted to Jewish matters and commits half of his time to them. Thanks to him, in Lvov, a committee was established and aid was organized. But there are problems in the committee. Dr. Diamand, a fervent Austrian patriot who is generally unhappy with the close ties to Jews from enemy Russia, opposed that Hausner had gone to Bobrinskii and requested his permission to organize a committee. Diamand called Hausner a traitor whose actions showed ingratitude to the Austrian government. Now that the committee is organized, he wants it to function independently of the Jewish gemina, so as not to compromise the gemina, and he refuses to serve as the committee's chairman.

Diamand is a very matter-of-fact, honest man, but he's an assimilationist who looks to the Poles and won't make a move without their approval. He is content to receive money from Russia, but only if it is unofficially distributed through the gemina. Hausner is a nationalist, practically a Zionist—a bold, very intelligent, and selfless man, but he's incredibly ambitious, is waging a struggle with Diamand, and wants the committee to function in an official manner. Apparently he wants to be the committee's chairman. But Diamand's position as the head of the Jewish gemina calls for him to be the chairman of such a committee. And the petty squabbles continue. Lander is completely on Hausner's side. I can't entirely make sense of this conflict and don't think it's our place to get mixed up in their internal affairs.

There is a copy of Sobiesky's charter to the Jews held here. But I didn't manage to see it. At night I returned to Lvov.

FEBRUARY 28

I saw two senior medical orderlies here who were from the State Duma Hospital in Tarnów, Khashavner (a Jew) and Putvinskii. In passing, Khashavner mentioned that in his presence an officer described having seen a Jew being led to headquarters. They ran across a Cossack. "Where are you taking him?" "To headquarters." "Why there? Run him through and be done!" Putvinskii was in Lvov during the pogrom in September. He saw Jews who were killed and wounded. He claims that six Cossacks were wounded by the civilian population.

MARCH 1

Leonid Andreev's sister had asked me by telephone back in Petrograd to seek out her brother, who was evacuated as a patient to Lvov, to give him some money that I would bring, and inform him that she was attempting to have him transferred to Petrograd. I searched for him in every hospital and couldn't find him. By chance, I learned today of the hospital where he was being treated and set off to see him. My help turned out to be unnecessary—just today his sister arrived from Petrograd to see him. But it was interesting to chat with him.

He's a young man with wonderful blue eyes and a transparent face that reveals a wasted, weary man. He recounted the terrible things he had endured. In passing, he said that in his presence, in the village of Libakhar, an officer named Dzentsuan Dzentsukhovskii arrested several Jews, beat them up, and sent them to headquarters. In order to spare them humiliation, more beatings and possibly getting killed along the way, Andreev took it upon himself to escort them. He delivered them to headquarters. But he doesn't know of their fate beyond that.

I saw Hausner. He proposed that I demand from Diamand the funds that were sent by the Petrograd Committee, that I tell him I need to distribute them. The purpose of this is so that the official Relief Committee, and not the gemina, will assume control of the funds. I categorically refused to resort to such tricks.

I ran into A. M. Khiriakov.[165] He's working for the Red Cross in Jarosław. He asked me to visit him. I have it in mind.

MARCH 2

I went to see Hausner. He implored me to go to Diamand and insist that he agree to join the Relief Committee and assume a role as its chairman. I was not eager to get involved in this affair, but I went to see him anyhow. My arrival caused a commotion, as it had when I visited Diamand the first time, until Diamand saw it was me and not an officer or a policeman. Diamand spoke of Hausner with great frustration, kept pointing out that a Relief Committee wasn't necessary; that the gemina, which is functioning as it had been earlier, can provide the necessary

aid; that for an Austrian subject to participate in a committee organized
by Russian Jews, and with the approval of the Russian governor general, is an act of ingratitude toward his government. He added that
Hausner is carrying on intrigues against him. I pointed out to him that
the Russians—the Petrograd and Kiev Relief Committees—cannot
send money otherwise, given what is legally required of those committees. They must have accountability that they can depend upon at
all times, and the committee allowed by Bobrinskii already exists. And
there is nothing illegal about this in relation to the Austrian government, since this is a purely charitable institution. We argued at length,
until he agreed, very reluctantly, to become the chairman of the committee.

Together with Hausner, I planned a route. Hausner insisted that my
first obligation was to go to the city of Stryi, where the population of
several thousand Jews, both in the town itself and in the vicinity, is literally starving to death. I agreed and left on a military transport train at
night. I settled into a standard heated car. There were no less than forty
people sitting there and it was completely crammed full of luggage. As
for a place to lie down, there was none to speak of. It was difficult even
to sit down. A number of people spent the whole night standing up. A
wounded officer found a spot near me. His wounds weren't healed, and
he was returning because there's a shortage of officers. There was one
woman sitting among us. The conductor demanded her papers. She
didn't have them, and he pulled her from the train. Even with my uniform, I was afraid as a civilian that he would ask for my papers too and
throw me out. But he didn't bother me.

We traveled the whole night, and I didn't sleep a wink.

MARCH 3

Stryi.[166] It's a rather decent little city. As in all the district[167] centers
(what we call provincial centers), there are many big buildings made
of stone, most of them public buildings, many beautiful ones. In several of the abandoned houses, horse stables had been set up, and
horse heads were protruding from their windows in a startling and
chilling way.

It was the same here as it was everywhere, of course. The Russians' arrival occurred without problems. But several months ago, the Russians left and the Austrians came, but stayed for only half a day. After they left, the Russians made a pogrom in the city. You can still feel a lot of tension in the city now. Military forces are moving intensely across the town, the wounded are being transported. You can hear heavy artillery fire now and then. The front is thirty to forty versts[168] from the city—and it seems as if all of this is a bivouac, as if our position is weak—one fateful move, and we'll have to retreat. And this tension is reflected in everything—it is expressed in the frightened expressions on the faces of Jews; in their timid and slavish bows; in that icons are displayed in the windows of every Christian home, as if a pogrom is expected at any minute. But the tense situation is especially revealed in the fact that the majority of shops are closed. The commandant posted announcements on the buildings stating that Jews are keeping their shops closed and, by doing so, are depriving the military sector of the ability to obtain essential items. In light of this, the commandant orders Jews to keep their shops open, including on Sabbaths and holidays. The failure to fulfill this order will be viewed as a boycott: violators will be fined, and the commandant will see to it that these shops are confiscated.

As I discovered, the condition that led the Jews to close their shops was this: the Russians were taking people for forced labor. They took one hundred men, Jews. At first, they went voluntarily. The Russians promised them each one ruble per day. But instead of paying them, the Cossacks who were charged with overseeing the work beat the workers, who ran away without getting paid. Then they began to seize Jews on the street, whoever appeared first in their sights, and send them to work. They even forced the elderly rabbi to work. The peasants wept when they saw the unfortunate old man. To avoid being rounded up, the Jews went to hide and didn't open their shops. The commandant summoned several community leaders to see him. He yelled at them, stamped his feet, screamed, "I'll deport you to Siberia!" The Jews calmly heard him out and said, "In Siberia there are laws too." He let them go at last, and then posted that announcement. The Jews offered one hundred men of their own and are paying them one gulden[169] a day out of their own funds and giving them bread. However, the seizure of Jews hasn't stopped altogether.

Went to the hotel. The owner is a Jewess. I talked with her. She described how the population here is suffering. Because of the prohibition of movement, there is terrible inflation; trade has totally come to a halt and there is a mass of starving people. The owner's daughter, who graduated from the conservatory in Vienna, is organizing concerts to benefit the poor.

I told the hotel owner that I wanted to meet one of the Jewish leaders here and said I had brought a sum of aid with me. She replied that the most respected leaders in the city—ten men, the rabbi among them—had been taken hostage and were being detained in a room inside the commandant's quarters. However, given the importance of my mission, she thinks it would be possible to arrange a meeting between us in one of the houses near the commandant's quarters. She called for someone right away and within an hour everything was arranged. A young man came for me and walked ahead of me. I followed him. He approached a small building across from the commandant's building and entered the vestibule. I lingered for a moment and then went in myself. The young man led me to an empty room. Soon four men walked in, one after another (the rabbi wasn't able to come). I told them why I had come. They told me they had previously formed a relief committee. Now, following the arrest of nearly all of the committee's members, the committee was forced to cease its activities. But because there as many as seven hundred families who are starving to death in the city and apart from the hostages there is no one who can possibly offer them help, the cell where they are sitting was gradually transformed into "the Committee." Hungry people come to them at the door and the window; the hostages somehow communicate with the more affluent people in town and also give their own money, down to their last dollar, and thus provide some relief to the starving people. But, of course, this is a drop in a sea.

Along with the Stryi hostages, there are also ten hostages under arrest from Sokal (Sokoliv). One of the latter, Appelgrin (who was fourth on my list), the owner of an enormous estate near Stryi, described how he had been ruined:

I used to own hundreds of cows, hundreds of horses, a large quantity of bread and other goods. The Russians came and took it all away. I rushed to see the commander to protest and he replied that they would pay for everything after the war. However, I did manage to retrieve seventy cows. They were taken again several days later. The peasants would drive in and show the soldiers where things were hidden, and in turn were given a share. Incidents like this took place: soldiers would pay someone for a cow or horse, but then return at night and take the money back at gunpoint.

At night, soldiers break into shops in the town square and take whatever they want. There were instances when the owners came out and raised an outcry. The soldiers would start to shoot and the owners would run to hide.

Appelgrin told a curious story about how he stayed in the city and didn't leave with others. "I was completely ready to leave for Vienna. But then at one point on the Sabbath, on the eve of my departure, I opened the midrash[170] and read an explanation of the place in the Bible where it says: 'and there was famine in the land, and Avram went to Egypt' (Genesis 12:10). In the explanation it is said that Avram was wrong to leave at a time when disaster struck the land. And I thought, disaster is about to strike our city too. Wouldn't it be wrong for me to leave? And I stayed behind with others."

In Lvov, there was a rumor going around that following the Austrians' second retreat from Stryi, Russian forces committed atrocities because the Jews denounced Russophiles to the Austrians, and the Russophiles were arrested or executed. "Nothing of the sort," my interlocutors declared. "We knew very well that the Russians could return, and we were awfully cautious in how we conducted ourselves. But the Ruthenians and Poles weren't shy—they openly informed on everyone to the Austrians. But the Jews tried to make themselves invisible and kept quiet."

"Here is what happened to me," one of them spoke up.

I own a flour warehouse. After the Russians arrived they started stealing from the warehouse. I hired five Cossacks and paid them each one ruble a day, and they guarded the warehouse. One time a Ruthenian who I know, a local, came by. He demanded twelve pounds of flour and shouted, "Yids! Your reign is over!" We weighed the flour for him. He took the flour and wanted to leave without paying. I stopped him: "And the money?" He began to argue again and refused to pay. He hurled the flour sacks to the floor, threatened to tear apart the store, and left.

A few days later the Austrians arrived. I was walking down the street, and that same Ruthenian was right in my path. Do you know what I did? I crossed the street to avoid running into him.

My interlocutors gave me information about towns and shtetls in the vicinity.

Chyrów and Felsztyn were demolished and burned. There are forty starving families in Lisiatycze, twenty-five in Bratkowce, one hundred in Sokołów. All of this is near Stryi, but doesn't include the Jews who are living in villages. Thus the needs in the neighboring cities and shtetls are indescribable.

I left that committee 1,500 rubles for Passover, both for Stryi and ten locations nearby, and promised to organize regular aid in the near future. We parted warmly and I left.

≈

I happened to find out that the Seventh Evacuation Hospital is located here, where Lev Nikolaevich Natanson, my niece's husband and brother of P. Natanson, is working as a doctor. I sought him out.

He's occupying some rooms in the house of a Jew who fled. There is still a completely ultra-Jewish atmosphere in the house, with books, a tallis, and tefillin. The house and all of its contents were confiscated, and within a few days, all of it will be transferred to the commandant. I took several of the more valuable old Jewish books and the tallis. And I felt some sense of guilt toward the rest of the books, which are awaited by a sad fate.

Natanson takes no interest whatsoever in Jewish matters; he even tries to keep his distance from them, and he's afraid. Indeed, and he's not alone. The majority of doctors, with the exception, of course, of the selfless F. E. Lander and to some extent Dr. Gilman, try to forget they're Jews and not remind others of this. It's cowardice of the most extreme kind. They're afraid to approach Jews, offer them help, or defend them; they're even afraid to transcribe a military circular that pertains to Jews. But when you bring up the subject of Jews with them, in order to clear their conscience, they allege that they never encountered any evidence of persecution of Jews, nor did they see any specific needs among Jews.

I asked Natanson to obtain a copy of the commandant's announcement about the Jewish shops for me. He claimed it was impossible.

He told me that more than ten thousand wounded had passed through their evacuation point alone, a mass of frostbitten extremities. The soldiers fight courageously. The officers display great heroism. There were cases when lightly wounded officers took some time before rejoining their regiments, and their colleagues wrote them insulting letters demanding that they not return. He also told me that six soldiers were shot for raping women.

I went to the rail station to find a train back to Lvov. At the station there were two trains, one behind another. In the first train, there was an echelon of soldiers leaving for the front, and a lively version of "Happy Nightingale" rang forth from there. In the second train, there were wounded men with frostbitten hands and feet, sick men, and moans were coming from there. And for a fleeting instant, it seemed the soldiers in the first train were utterly unaware of what was happening inside the one behind them, that it was being concealed from them, and that had they known, all of their happiness would have vanished at once.

At the station, there was a hospital train going to Lvov and I rode back with it.

MARCH 4

Went to see Hausner. Told him about Stryi. I was about to leave, but he held me back. Just then a man from the gemina arrived with 8,000 rubles. Hausner loudly said, "Here, the money for you has been delivered!" He called the man over, took the money from him, asked me to count it, and suggested that I sign a receipt for it. I didn't understand anything and refused to sign. He signed for it himself. Finally I understood. It seems Hausner requested the money from Diamand in order to give it to me and to demonstrate proof of this he staged this farce in front of the other man. This profoundly bothered me, and I said to him:

"Why have you embroiled this clerk in our affairs? Why did you have
to invite him over while I was here?"

"An-sky, he is a grave."

"Nonetheless, I prefer not to be part of this grave. And in general, I
don't want you to involve me in your relationships with Diamand and
the gemina."

≈

I saw Bonch-Osmolovskii.[171] Together with Vidrina and another young
man, he came here to run a food supply division for the Pirogov Society[172] and Free Economic Society.[173] In Rava-Ruska and Magerov, they
opened meal stations and ambulatory clinics, for which they hired
young Austrian physicians, mostly Jews. In addition to the distribution
of aid, they aim to follow the principle of being "without distinction of
nationality" in their work. They find themselves waging a great struggle, not only with the local authorities, but also with the Christian population, which can't come to terms with the thought that Jews might be
accorded help equally with others.

Bonch-Osmolovskii established ties to Count V. Bobrinskii[174] and his
committee, and that committee promised to support the Pirogov Society division by supplying it with food. Bonch-Osmolovskii still depends
in a significant way on a subsidy from the Jewish Relief Committee and
was asking for my assistance with this. I promised to think about it.

At night, I met with one of the local women, Shvebt, who is working
to provide aid to the population, and she complained that hard-working
women are forbidden from joining the Relief Committee, and no one
takes their opinions into account.

She told me that five soup kitchens that serve 4,500 people were established here: at Tikvat Zion,[175] 2,000 are served; at Yad Kharutzim,[176]
1,400. At two locations (for the intelligentsia), six hundred; and at one
for skilled workers, five hundred.

In addition, the gemina distributes two kilos of bread to individuals
each week, to 1,700 people.

The municipal government gives out clothing and supplies to the
wives of reservists, but very little reaches the Jews, and hardly any of the
clothes. A subsidy of 1,500 rubles for a Jewish trade school was received

from Petrograd. A shelter for two hundred children was set up, and it was proposed that they build one for another two hundred. They are organizing shelters for girls who need to be protected from prostitution. There is one Mrs. Raikhenshtein, a very cultured woman, who is involved with this; the Petrograd Committee promised to give 2,500 or 1,500 rubles a month for this project.

MARCH 5

Relations between Hausner and Diamand are growing ever more complicated. The committee isn't becoming official or getting organized, the aid work isn't moving ahead, and money isn't being distributed to the provinces. It's essential to put pressure on the relief workers here. In order to do this, I need to meet with Lander.

I went to Zholkva today to talk it over with Lander, and together we decided to insist that all the issues must finally be resolved.

In Zholkva, the atmosphere is generally calm. Jewish autonomy has been maintained there, but because of Russification politics, the commandant forbade the publication of books in Polish.

"In which language should we publish them, then? We don't know Russian, after all."

"Publish them in Hebrew or Yiddish," is how the commandant resolved the matter.[177]

And the books are being published in Hebrew.

The city received money to aid the civilian population. The Relief Committee that was founded here decided not to give aid to the Jews. The Jews are rich. But the Jews managed to stand up for themselves and a small sum was allotted to them too.

A police constable described the terrible things that befell Jewish landowners. An order was issued that when a pogrom begins on an estate, it is to be immediately halted with the most severe measures. But if the estate is Jewish, then report this to High Command and wait for instructions . . . Because the peasants kiss landowners' hands, and used to also kiss the hands of Jewish landowners, there were cases that Jewish landowners were forced to kiss Ruthenians' bare backsides. As for Jewish estates being totally pillaged, this is a given. It's the system.

A Jewish family was shot and killed by artillerists not far from Zholkva. Lander described the terrible spread of prostitution in Lvov. The troops have shamed and infected a mass of girls with syphilis, who are now infecting others. And now there are cries that Jewish prostitutes are infecting the army.

At the train station where I waited for the train for several hours, there was a soldier rolling around in an unconscious state in the dirt who was drunk on denatured alcohol. He was deliriously shouting, grinding his teeth.

"Give me a knife! I . . . I need a knife! I'll cut the Germans. . . . Cut off my leg! Cut it! Ah—ah—aaah . . ."

It was terrible to watch him and listen to that bloody prattle.

I rode back to Lvov. There was a Pole in the train compartment, and he was giving speeches: "A Pole can't accomplish anything without a Jew, nor can a Jew accomplish anything without a Pole. A Pole needs someone to lie to him, and a Jew needs someone to lie to."

MARCH 6

Lvov. I proposed to Bonch-Osmolovskii that I join his division and distribute aid to Jews in that capacity from the Jewish Relief Committee's funds. He refused. Even without me, his Pirogov Society division is considered "Jewish." The division shouldn't stray from the principle of being "without distinction of religion."

"If that's so," I said to him, "then why do you turn to the Jewish Committee for help? If that's so, then apply your principles to the manner in which you acquire money. Take money without distinction of religion. Otherwise you'll get money from Jews and distribute the aid 'without distinction.'"

But we didn't settle on anything. Vidrina drew a gloomy picture of starving Jews who are living in Magerov and other burned cities. They're living in pits and dugouts. Here in Lvov, the soup kitchens will be closed for Passover. This is utter nonsense.

MARCH 7

I saw in the registry that one Baron Gintsburg is staying in the hotel. I thought Vladimir Goratsievich had come and stopped by his room. In fact it was Alfred Goratsievich,[178] the only Jewish officer in the Russian Army. I spoke with him. He told me several facts concerning the slander of Jews.

Tomorrow I leave for Lubaczów, Jarosław, Rzeszów, and other places.

MARCH 8

I'm in a train car. I'm riding the Gentry Organization's hospital train. There are a few officers there, and the conversation concerns the so-called Wild Division the whole time. People speak about their conduct and savageries as if they were charming pranks. A nurse who seems to be from the aristocracy tenderly describes how a "Wild" man hauled off a stolen sewing machine. Much of what is said about them is typical and curious: they don't subscribe to any form of discipline. They sleep without a watchman. If you bring this up with them, they reply, "if you're afraid, post a watchman—we aren't afraid." Their first question: "Who do we cut?"

One of the officers spoke very sincerely about fear. During his first battle, he momentarily fell unconscious from fear. Now he has grown used to it.

The officers brought up Jews too, of course. They occupied a village. They seized an old Jew, brought him to headquarters. He seemed suspicious. They began interrogating him, he knew nothing. A colonel ordered his arrest. They led him to a hut and left him there. That night he asked them to take him to the colonel and said, "Captain sir, such-and-such house here is filled with weapons." They went and did indeed find a house packed with weapons and a telephone in the cellar. "What should we do with the old man?" they asked the colonel. "To hell with him, let him go." And they released him.

"Our forces captured some small town," another said.

The soldiers went to search it. A soldier walked inside one house and an old sick Jew was lying there, moaning, about to die at any second. The soldier was about to leave when all of a sudden he heard the characteristic "tick"—something clicked. He turned around and began searching, and in the bed of the supposedly dying man he found a telephone.

And then in another place, two artillery officers appeared in a small town at the border with Lublin province. They were asking everyone questions and looking everything over, and no one had a clue as to who they were. They seemed suspicious and were arrested. They turned out to be Germans. At the interrogation, they informed that their accomplice was an Orthodox priest whom they paid 12,000 rubles to conceal them and show them how to get to the army. All three of them were hanged.

We reached Lubaczów[179] late at night. After exiting the station I didn't know which direction to take to get to town. I asked a passerby. A lieutenant colonel who was walking behind me heard my question and called out, "Let's go, I'm walking to town too."

We went. "Where are you going?" he asked.

"To a hotel," I replied, not knowing how to respond.

"My God, are you mad? A hotel, here?" he exclaimed, laughing. "The whole city is almost entirely in ruins!"

"What should I do?"

"Go and see the commandant. He'll let you know where to spend the night. Let's go, I'll show you where he lives."

I had no reason to go to the commandant, since I had nothing to say to him to about why I was there. Nevertheless, we went. We approached the main square, and it was a complete wreck. There were remnants of burned houses and trading stalls. "What caused the fire? Was there a battle here?" I asked my escort.

"A battle? This was the Cossacks out marauding. And mind you," he added, "they acted with discretion: They set only the Jews' houses on fire. Wherever a house is intact it belongs to a Christian. They burned nearly all of the Jewish ones."

"But why?" I asked.

"For no reason at all. Just because. To punish the yids."

He pointed out the commandant's house to me from a distance and went off in a different direction himself.

Instead of going to the commandant, I entered the first shop I came across, which turned out to be Jewish, of course. I talked with the people, asked them where I could buy leather. They led me to one house.

In a large room, there were several pairs of shoes, boots, and pieces of leather hanging along the walls. These were the remnants of a large leather business. Two families are living in that room, twelve souls. The owner, an elderly, dignified Jewess, tearfully told me: "We were wealthy;

we owned a large shoe and leather store. The soldiers burned the whole thing to ashes. Whatever you see here is what remains. Right when they entered the city they began dousing Jewish houses and shops in kerosene and setting them on fire. They looted at the time, of course. They were stationed near

[FIRST DIARY FRAGMENT ENDS HERE.]

TWO

Fall 1915

Petrograd

[SECOND DIARY FRAGMENT RESUMES HERE.]

SEPTEMBER 9

. . . a Russian-language newspaper. Katz responded reasonably, that as long as the government bars the Jews from entering Russian schools, the government can say nothing to him about the harm of Yiddish language, or the Jews' duty to attach themselves to Russian culture. Volzhin[1] replied that Baron A. G. Gintsburg[2] and M. A. Varshavskii[3] also told him they consider all the various types of publications in Yiddish to be harmful. Could they really have said something of that sort to Volzhin?

SEPTEMBER 10

I went to see Sliozberg. He finally drew up a complete petition on my behalf; I signed it and he promised to deliver it to Shcherbatov[4] tomorrow.

Gorky had planned to visit and meet with me about the *Anthology,* but he came down with bronchitis and didn't come.

I went to see K. V. Nikolaevskii[5] (after having visited Pozner on the same floor). I didn't catch him. I did catch Nina Nikolaevna and Olga.

FIGURE 2.1. Military petition parade in Petrograd, September 9, 1915. *Courtesy of the* YIVO *Institute for Jewish Research, New York.*

Nina Nikolaevna is a simple woman; with drawn lips, she speaks rapidly and in a monotone, like a chatterbox, and all the while maintains a frozen expression on her face. She speaks with the tone of someone who is extremely certain, but is always repeating others' words, like a parrot. She began telling me that all of the troops she has met unanimously said that in the theater of war all spies are Jews. The Germans always know about everything, and this is because Jews inform them with all kinds of signals and underground telephones. The Cossacks deal harshly with Jews, but they can't be restrained. They've gotten so infuriated with Jewish espionage that they simply can't control themselves. I gave her my opinion about the claims of alleged Jewish espionage, German intelligence, and motives for Cossack reprisals. She agreed with me at once and began to prattle on about Germans. The real problem is that Germans who are on the inside have seized control of everything and are traitors to the army. But the Jews? How can they know what's happening? But there are Germans throughout the Russian Army and they can't be gotten rid of. Here is a "fact:" a regiment received an order to walk to one location. They marched quickly, without the usual breaks. And their colonel, a German, drove behind them in a car. It seemed suspicious to the soldiers that they were being transferred so rapidly, and they asked the officers to send scouts ahead of them. The officers said, "We don't have an order from the colonel for that." But the soldiers insisted on stopping and driving the scouts ahead. Well, the officers agreed. They stopped and sent the scouts. Half an hour later, the scouts came running to the battalion commander: "Your Honor, you must come with us and look with your own eyes at the location to which we were being driven." He went with them. He walked ahead a few steps and saw German wire barriers and a battery straight ahead and to either side: they had been lying in wait for the regiment to walk into their trap and start firing at it from all directions. They came back running, waving their arms: "Turn around!" Just then the colonel drove up in a car, shouting, "Why have you stopped?" They told him they had sent scouts ahead. He got nasty: "Who allowed this? Step forward at once!" Two officers then approached him with their sabers drawn and demanded that he depart with them for headquarters. They led him to headquarters and reported all of it, then returned by themselves to their units. A month passed. The regiment was transferred and stationed in another location next to a different regiment. And suddenly the officers saw that their colonel, the one they arrested, was commanding that other regiment. And here's why you can't get rid of Germans.

"I went to visit a hospital," she said.

Both the soldiers and officers there had the same worry: Germans. They would say things such as, "All of them are spies and ought to be exterminated." I would say to them that you mustn't judge everyone like that. Some of them simply have German names, but in fact are Russian souls. But they would counter that by saying, "There are none like that. A German name means you're already a traitor." I would say to them, "But so many of them are dying in the Russian Army! Just read the obituaries of the dead who have German names in the *New Times*."[6] My interlocutors didn't say anything but just glanced at me sort of strangely. But after some time passed and we grew closer, one called me over and said, "You were talking a little while back here about German officers who fell in battle. That's not really the case. They don't exist . . ." "How can that be! There are countless numbers of them!" I exclaimed. He smiled slyly and said, "There are obituaries about them, but they were killed for other reasons—not because they fought for Russia." "How then?"

He leaned in and said, "We shoot them ourselves. It's the same everywhere. A German? Finish him off. And as soon as the fighting starts, shoot him first."

And if she omitted a large part of the story, that too would have been typical.

At night I went to see Tsinberg.[7] We spoke about the legions.[8] He began with the thought that it's senseless, but concluded that it's a good, only a risky, endeavor.

SEPTEMBER 12

Yesterday and today, Sliozberg was still making promises: "That's right, I'll take care of it tomorrow." I have finally grown tired of this, and told him today that it seems he hasn't the time to deal with this and I'm turning to Varshavskii. He began to insist that he would do it without further delay. But I took the petition back from him. Tomorrow I will go to see Varshavskii.

I visited Vengerov[9] to ask him to speak with Batiushkov[10] about my play. He replied that he would gladly do this, but did not expect that it would show at the Aleksandrinskii. After Iushkevich's[11] play *Mendel'*

Spivak was staged there, the director received a telegram from the Grand Duke (I don't remember which one): to what had the Aleksandrinskii Theater come if it was staging a Jewish play. "In general," he said, "in order to write a good play you need to have talent; to stage it, you need to be a genius."

He complained to me in passing that his son, who was born after he, Semyon Afanasievich, had already converted, was not being promoted to officer. I did not express any sympathy. He asked me to give him my autobiography for the publication of *Twentieth Century Writers*.[12] It will include a separate section about Russian-Jewish writers, where he'll put me, Aizman,[13] and Iushkevich. The latter was unhappy that he of all people would be isolated from the Russian writers. "Why are you putting me in a mass grave?" was how he phrased it.

≈

At night I attended an evening in memory of Lutugin.[14] I went there with a considerably higher opinion of Lutugin than the one that I left with afterward. The speeches were either lifeless, hysterical, or else phony. People lauded his geographical work, his humorous attitude to everyday life. In regard to his social activism, they said he switched from one party to another, that he didn't have an ideology. Who was he, really?

Shmaryahu Levin[15] once told me: "A woman was asked: 'Which is your husband—a Cohen, Levi, or Israel?'[16] She replied, 'He's a tinsmith, but he's a very good man.'"

That anecdote unwittingly came to my mind.

SEPTEMBER 13

I went to see M. A. Varshavskii. He's a relic of his own kind, a *moykhes*.[17] No one puts any stock in his opinions about social matters, but when a representative or someone to accompany a delegation is needed, they choose him. For him, as for A. G. Gintsburg, this is a tradition that he inherited from his parents, who were rightfully regarded as renowned leaders of the Jews. According to tradition, M. A. displays great patriotism—he enjoys visiting the ministers and sends them telegrams that express his loyalty as a representative of the community.

Varshavskii assured me he considers it a duty and a pleasure to intervene on my behalf for a residence permit. He asked that I deliver the petition to him tomorrow.

≈

I visited Jabotinsky's[18] house. One man who was there just returned from Stockholm and said the speeches about the legions that Jabotinsky gave in Copenhagen[19] and Stockholm stirred up a lot of debates. The man brought a number of American newspapers in Russian, including one from Argentina. There is a pro-Russian bias in them.

Babkov[20] informed me that Betzalel[21] definitively refused to host my lecture about the legions.

≈

I received a call from someone on the telephone. It turned out to be S. M. Shryro,[22] from Baku. He's a rather odd, eccentric man. He was born in the shtetl Oshmiany and used to be a poor *yeshibotnik*,[23] and his originality consists in that despite having become a millionaire, he has remained the same *yeshibotnik*, with all of his mannerisms, ignorance of Russian language, and lack of culture. But then, he's preserved a certain measure of *yeshibotnik*-like idealism—the capacity to get fired up and captivated. It is true that for him this is connected with ambition, with giving charity. But a considerable amount of heart goes into that too. And because of this, he stands above many other cultural activists. He's a territorialist in his outlook, and this matter has cost him a great deal of money. Now he has grown disappointed in this as well. His first words to me over the telephone were, "Is it true you've lost your mind?" And he explained he meant my advocacy of the legions. I replied to him that I had no interest in speaking with him about this.

In the evening, he and his brother came to visit me. He was recounting how in London, from where he recently returned, he was subjected to an inquisitorial interrogation: what was he doing there? Why did he send 25,000 francs to his family in Switzerland? In short, for two hours, they elicited information about all the trivialities of his life. He also said that in London, the censorship is stricter than it is here. Uttering a word against Russia is forbidden. The newspapers weren't allowed to print Deputy Fridman's speech,[24] which was printed in Russian newspapers, because the shameful treatment of Jews in Russia is mentioned in that speech.

Shryro touched on the question of the legions twice, but I didn't respond. At one point, in response to my remark that the social activist S. is someone who in theory ought to sympathize with the idea of the legions, he even noted, "He's too foolish for that."

Then Shryro's brother asked me to explain the idea and purpose of the legions to him. I was rather annoyed, and in a few heated words, I stated my legionist credo. S. M. Shryro listened intently to me. It was evident that I made an impression on him. And when I finished, he resolutely declared:

"Well, here it is: After tomorrow I will write you a check for 1,000 rubles, for the publicity of this cause. And if it happens that England provides some kind of guarantee, I will dedicate my entire fortune to it."

It was a positively beautiful gesture. But a half an hour or perhaps an hour later, it was clear that he was regretful—not because of the money, but rather because he was embarrassed that he had gotten carried away, and he started to prove that this is all a chimera, that you can't depend on Jabotinsky's word. But he didn't renege on his promise.

SEPTEMBER 14

I delivered the petition to Varshavskii and he promised to get it into Shcherbatov's hands today or tomorrow, either personally, or through a close friend of the minister, who is on a first-name basis with Shcherbatov.

SEPTEMBER 15

At night, the [Jewish] political plenum convened. The whole night there were debates about the rights of the plenum and the Political Bureau. All of them concluded with the idea that the plenum ought to select an executive committee, whose main job will be to prod the bureau to take action. Sliozberg was anxious, nervous, hysterical. He saw in this an infringement on his own authority. He claimed that the plenum has no rights of any kind. Toward the end of the debates, I said a few words: "We've spoken the whole time here about the plenum's rights, and have said nothing about its duties. I propose that its rights ought to flow from its duties. But what have the plenum's members accomplished over these past fifteen months? Have they taken the least bit of interest in seeing for themselves what is happening to Jewry?"

It seems my words made an impression; at least, that's what I was told.

At the end of the meeting, G. B. Sliozberg reported on his discussion with the minister of National Education[25] regarding the subject of admission for all Jews who wish to enter institutions of higher learning, but [who] can't be admitted under the quotas. The minister agreed with him that in principle the quota ought to be removed, that it would be ideal if any person who has the right could be admitted to the university, but he pointed out that there isn't a place for everyone. Given that the number of Jewish students has grown to several thousand in the past ten years, a quota for Russians would become necessary. Sliozberg pointed out the possibility of the provincial universities to him.

There was also a discussion with Shcherbatov about the further expansion of several places in the Pale, and Shcherbatov agreed to some of this.[26]

People say there were serious disturbances in Moscow. People have been killed and wounded.

There is news of a major French victory. Could this signal the start of an Allied advance on the Western Front?

SEPTEMBER 16

I received the check for 1,000 rubles from Shryro.

I asked Sasha Viktorovna Gurevich to organize a reading of my play at her home, with tickets, to benefit the legions. She agreed to it, albeit not very eagerly.

SEPTEMBER 17

I've given up on organizing readings of the play. It will provoke rumors and gossip. I have to explain its point to each and every person. It isn't worth it.

Gershman, a legionist from Moscow, said that a few days ago in Moscow Ussishkin[27] gave a thunderous speech against the legions; he referred to the Aleksandrinskii Legion as the "Asinine Legion," and blackened Jabotinsky's name, of course.

Gershman said that intense rioting took place in Moscow. A policeman was killed at Lesner's factory. Many civilians were killed and wounded.

I'm leaving for Moscow. Khodotov[28] gave me a very passionate letter for Sanin,[29] a director at Sukhodolskii's Theater.

≈

Just before my departure, Varshavskii telephoned me. "Congratulations! You've been given a residence permit for six months."

This news brought me little happiness. "Just six months? Chlenov[30] told me that Obolensky[31] promised me a residence permit to last through the end of the war. But I made the request before the Jewish laws were revised."

"Well, don't worry. That doesn't matter now. Now they've given one to you for six months, and they'll give another," he replied.

It's a pity that I got involved with these intercessors. I should have asked Shingaryov,[32] or Batiushkov, through the Literary Society. Yes, I forgot. Yesterday, Varshavskii asked me over the phone if I was acquainted with a legal deputy who could intercede on my behalf. I coldly replied that I was not acquainted with such a deputy, nor would I run to such a person for help.

SEPTEMBER 20

I spent two days in Moscow. Sanin, who is short, round, middle-aged, a Jew or of Jewish descent, received me well, was interested in the play that Khodotov's letter had described, and arranged a reading for the following day in the presence of all the directors. "However, the timing is unfortunate," he added. "We just accepted a play by Andreev, and four plays by Naidenov, A. Tolstoy, Iushkevich, and another has been 80 percent accepted. Nonetheless, we will listen to your play. But what is this utterly new, never-before-described existence about which Nikolai Nikolaevich (Khodotov) writes?"

"It's from the life of the Jews—mystics, hasids, and *tsadiks*," I replied.

"Ah, so that's what it is . . ." and he knit his brow. "And what is the subject?"

I told him in a few words. The furrows on his brow grew deeper.

"Yes . . . this is very interesting, but not at all suited to the present moment. Right now the public right is looking for joyful, light fare, so as not to see or hear what is happening—so as to forget all about these scum (he named names). But your play is heavy. . . . If you wish, we will read it, but I am certain beforehand that it will not work. If you can spare the time, we will read it tomorrow . . ."

I took my leave.

That evening I spoke with I. V. Johnson. He had spoken with L. A. Sulerzhitskii,[33] who read my play last year for the Art Theater and gave several directions. Now I have revised it according to his instructions. We arranged to read it the next day. I read it yesterday. Sulerzhitskii found it satisfactory as a whole, but pointed out that the first act in which the love of Khonen and Leah ought to clearly emerge was lacking. As it is, one can only guess about it.

I refused to add an act, but promised to add features throughout the first act that would convey the love between the young people. I will inform Sulerzhitskii once I have done this, and he will set up a general reading and summon me by telegram.

It seems that there were serious disturbances in Moscow. They began when a conductor threw a drunken Georgievskii Cavalry soldier off of a tram. A crowd stepped in to defend the soldier, the police showed up, fighting broke out, and shots were fired into the crowd. Thirteen people were evidently killed as a result, and thirty-two wounded.

≈

While I was at the Union of Towns, I saw E. L. Gurevich-Stirnov.[34] He told me the newspaper venture has fallen into disarray. The Populists aren't contented with the fact that the editor will be one of their own (apparently A. V. Peshekhonov[35]) and demanded that Populists constitute the majority of the editorial board. But they easily reached a consensus in regard to the paper's ideology.

≈

I left almost straight from the train station today for a committee meeting at the [Jewish] Historical-Ethnographic Society.[36] Here is a scholarly society indeed. It hardly takes notice of the war and is preoccupied with its own internal affairs: whether to publish a book in one or two volumes.

I raised the question of what measures the society adopted to preserve objects of Jewish antiquity, which in the most barbaric ways have throughout the Pale been annihilated, pillaged, and reduced in this war. Hundreds of synagogues—storehouses of Jewish artifacts— have been destroyed. It seems the one thing they did was to go to the Ethnographic Society at the Academy of Sciences, with a request that it place old Jewish synagogues that possess archeological value under its auspices. The Academy of Sciences replied that as a rule this falls outside the scope of its activities. I proposed that we instruct a plenipotentiary from the Jewish Relief Committee to organize the evacuation of the more valuable sacred objects in each location and remove the objects themselves wherever possible. I promised to compile a list.

After the meeting, I went to see Varshavskii. A great disappointment awaited me there. Apparently the six-month residence permit was not yet given to me, but merely promised; meanwhile, my request was sent to the Department of Police, and from there will go to the Division of Security for further information. And from there, a reply will be given that I lived abroad for fifteen years and am considered a revolutionary writer. And thus once again my "right of residence" will be buried for a long time to come.

During the day, the Literary Society[37] committee held a meeting. The question of lectures was discussed. They suggested that I lecture about my impressions of the war. Instead I proposed that I lecture about "activism"[38]—about the need for Jews to step forward in this war under a national banner, as a nation, and make a claim to their historic homeland—that is, about the legions. The committee's members frowned and looked wary, but couldn't fail to see that it is an exciting issue, and they agreed, asking only that I speak about the topic more broadly, and not specifically about the legions. I forgot to mention above that I lectured about the legions a week ago to young party intellectuals (SS, KS, Bundists).[39] I spoke lethargically during the first half of the lecture, but more energetically during the second. There were debates, but no objections based on purely socialist principles were raised. I lectured again today in someone's home, mainly for socialist youth from that same Betzalel group that wasn't able to host my lecture.

Prior to giving the lecture, I visited Gorky at his apartment at 23 Kronverskii Prospekt. He recently moved there and the apartment is still unfurnished. This is the second time I am seeing Gorky, and I can't come to grips with his appearance. He is a workman from head to toe. His features have grown neither softer nor more refined. He still has the same absurdly squashed and truncated nose, a forehead slashed with deep wrinkles; not the face of a cultured man but of a worker, gigantic hands, a habit of stressing the "o." But then what creates a wonderful face are his eyes, which are blue, kind and clear, and his fleetingly gentle, affectionate, and tender smile.

We spoke about the *Anthology*. He wants it to be literary and social at the same time. The way he conceives of the content and character of the articles involved is especially vague. I suggested that rather than offering three folios of articles, there ought to be just three articles: one about Jewish literature as a reflection of daily life and internal developments, a second about literature and the external conditions of Jewish life, and a third about literature from an aesthetic point of view. I suggested that we delegate the writing of these essays to Eliashev,[40] Niger,[41] and Tsinberg. He agreed to this, and I offered to talk it over with Tsinberg.

It seems Gorky had been warned about my attitudes toward the legions. He told me: "Jabotinsky wrote a letter to me, wanting to meet with me, but there was a misunderstanding. When he arrived at the time I had called for, the porter mistakenly told him I wasn't home. He left a letter for me, in which he asks: first, that I make a statement about the question of Jews who are fighting for Palestine; second, that I write to a number of European writers, like D'Annunzio,[42] Shaw,[43] Wallace[44] and others, asking them to state their views about this question. I would be glad to write these letters, but I think the list is rather random. When you see Jabotinsky, send me a longer list and I'll write to all of them. When it comes to making a personal statement, I must refrain from doing so. I have particular views on this count. I am genuinely glad, for example, that the Pan-Slavic idea, which I detest, has been finally extinguished by Bulgaria's entry into the war against the Allies. How then can I make a statement about the Palestine question?"

"Didn't you once come out in defense of Zionism in an article?"

"I have been reminded of that article three times now. I don't recall it and didn't see it in print. I remember writing a letter to someone from Riga in which I stated my views about Zionism. I don't recall anything else."

I promised to get him that article, which was printed in a *Pravda*[45] pamphlet.

He asked for the opportunity to hear my lecture at the Literary Society next Sunday and will then respond. I promised to invite him to the lecture.

≈

At night, I gave another lecture about the Legions. This time I spoke with great inspiration. Several people told me they had come there as enemies and were leaving as friends, that I won them over. There were many debates, all of them concerned with the fear of the risk involved and the notion that this is not a Jewish matter. People also pointed out that England wouldn't give anything, that there could be German legions. But the only one to argue against the basic principle was Tsinberg, who claimed that Jews (in the Diaspora) have never taken up the sword, and that their strength lies in this.

I responded with everyone present and was told it was a convincing response.

SEPTEMBER 21

I went to see Gorky at the Parus publishing house[46] to make definitive arrangements for the *Anthology*. I spoke with him in regard to my work

"A Jewish Apocalypse" (10 Signs),[47] which Pozner told me Gorky had read and enjoyed. In fact he hadn't read it. I read it for him. It was evident that he didn't particularly like it. He offered to give it to the editors at *The Contemporary*.[48]

SEPTEMBER 22

Last night, I ran into Naidich, who was here on a trip. When I told him about my ordeals with the residence permit he was bowled over. Instead of arranging a residence permit for me, something that Varshavskii could have easily done, he needlessly ruined it. I need to find out to whom he gave the petition. Today I went to see Varshavskii. At first he didn't want to tell me to whom he had given the petition. Then he said: "To Putilov, assistant director of the Department of Public Affairs." Putilov is Naidich's acquaintance, but has a lower rank of authority. Shcherbatov could have signed the request without any sort of further information. But, of course, Putilov had to send it to the Department of Police. Naidich talked it over with Putilov, who told him that nothing can be done now until the Department of Police responds.

≈

I went to see Sliozberg. He asked about my right of residence, and I said that instead of receiving help, I was harmed. I had come to see him about a different matter. I asked him to introduce a question to the Political Bureau for consideration: which measures to adopt, so that during the anticipated retreat of the German Army (which I think will indeed happen, although not quickly), Russian military forces, especially Cossacks, do not subject those towns and shtetls that the Germans occupied to ravages and plunder—so that what happened in Kuzhi, Orany[49] and other places (slander and executions without trial) is not repeated. We must take some sort of measures in advance.

Sliozberg was inert as he listened to me, and then impatiently replied, "Well, what can we do? We can't do anything."

SEPTEMBER 24

Following Naidich's advice, I met with L. M. Aizenberg.[50] Yesterday over the phone, Putilov promised Naidich he would give me a temporary residence permit until the Department of Police clears it and asked for Aizenberg to speak with him. Aizenberg went to see him today, and Putilov reneged on his promise.

≈

Rumor of a change in leadership. Three new ministers will be appointed: Kryzhanovskii,[51] Khvostov,[52] and ... Muratov.[53]

SEPTEMBER 25

At another meeting with Aizenberg, Putilov requested that he bring him some of my books, so he can see I am in fact a writer and not a hack (his words).

I went to see Gornfeld.[54] He told a story about Muizhel.[55] The latter is a terrible liar. During a conversation with Miakotin,[56] he took offense to something and exclaimed, "Are you comparing me with Nemirovich-Danchenko?" To this Miakotin calmly replied, "I am not comparing you. I think *Russian Word*[57] is a better newspaper than *Stock Market Gazette*,[58] and Nemirovich a more talented writer than you." Muizhel was terribly hurt.

Gornfeld talked about Kipen.[59] Moscow Association is publishing his collected works.

The sister of the policeman Markovich, whom I had connected with the Union of Zemstvos in Warsaw last year (see my diary), came by to see me. She has been working this whole time, for seven months in Błonie, and now in Bobriusk. A hard-working girl. She put up and is still putting up with a lot from the Poles who are working for the union.

SEPTEMBER 26

Grzhebin[60] promised to run my play by the censor. He's very close with Baron Drizen.[61]

SEPTEMBER 27

It's over. What we expected has become a fact. Shcherbatov left, and A. N. Khvostov, the fervent Judeophobe and Rightist, was appointed in his place. Samarin[62] left as well. This is because of Rasputin's protégé Varnava.[63]

We received news about the horrors that took place in Smorgon. After the enemy occupied the city, before which time it underwent relatively little damage, the Germans went on a rampage, snatching watches, boots, and shoes from people. But the Russians returned and retook the city. The Germans withdrew but continued fighting back. A battle took place right in the city and bombs exploded. The population hid in cellars. When the Cossacks there realized they wouldn't be able to hold the city, they expelled all of the residents from their homes that night and set fire to the city from all sides. They were given half an hour before being forced to leave, without being able to take anything with them. And so a population of forty thousand people fled from the city in the pitch-black night, under heavy enemy fire, as a sea of flames consumed the city. Many people were burned alive, many were killed, and many died on the road. For an entire week, they drifted 110 versts[64] toward Minsk. This is how in half an hour's time, a prosperous industrialized city died, everyone became a pauper, and many also became corpses.

I lectured today at the Literary Society. More than four hundred people attended and more than one hundred people weren't able to come. I spoke passionately. They listened with keen interest. When I reached the point of repudiating the Zionists' worries, Chairman Kreinin[65] stopped me. But then he was also stopping my opponents, who wanted to debate the whole Zionist platform. The opposition was unbelievably feeble; there was just one Chemerinskii at whom critics and the audience were shouting, "Enough!" Because of the late hour, several speakers didn't have time to make statements, and even I had only ten minutes to respond. But I did what I needed to do. People will be up in arms, and they will grow accustomed to the idea that Jews can go out with weapons in their hands in defense of their national rights.

Yesterday while accompanying Markovich to the train station, I ran into Khurgin and his brother-in-law, Dr. Blokh, who is going to Tarnopol. I insisted that Blokh take some money with him for the Galician Jews. Khurgin promised to give him several hundred rubles, and I will repay him here from the Relief Committee's funds.

FIGURE 2.2. Minsk Street, Smorgon, after being destroyed during the occupations of the Russian and German armies, 1918. *Courtesy of the* YIVO *Institute for Jewish Research, New York.*

I ran into Peshekhonov at the train station. He's leaving for Moscow to take care of the newspaper. It's on track again.

SEPTEMBER 28

Grinboym,[66] the Zionist, (from Warsaw), came to see me. He's joining the editorial board of a newspaper here (a Zionist one) and asked me to contribute. I didn't give a definitive promise. We spent a long time arguing about the legions.

People are talking about Shcherbatov's report regarding the resolutions from the Unions of Towns and Zemstvos meeting,[67] saying that it was proposed that he invite Prince Lvov[68] and Chelnokov[69] to see him, so as to relay gratitude to them for their productive work, and to indicate to them that because the unions have stepped outside the bounds of their authorized work, their delegation cannot be received.

Shcherbatov did this, but during the course of a long discussion, Chelnokov and Lvov managed to win him over, and he left their meeting with a new line. His conclusion was to resign. Samarin's resignation on account of Rasputin and Varnava made a shocking impression in Moscow.

SEPTEMBER 29

Yaakov Lvovich Neitel came to see me. He had recently arrived from London; conveyed greetings from Jabotinsky. He doesn't share Jabotinsky's views, but being a good man, he likes Jabotinsky, and as a friend is willing to help. But then again, he likes everyone and is willing to help everyone.

I gave a lecture at the Psycho-Neurological Institute; there were three hundred to four hundred students, both men and women. I felt inspired as I spoke. The debates were passionate and crossed the line at times into hysterics. Party leaders spoke out, especially the Bundists. I had to fight on two fronts: Zionists and Bundists. A Russian got mixed up in the debates and, while banging on a table, was shouting that Jews must go to the revolution. It made a painful impression.

In general, the meeting yielded dozens of followers.

At night a group of legionists held a gathering. We decided to establish a party. We elected a commission to draw up a statute.

SEPTEMBER 30

I met with Naidich and Aizenberg. The two of them decided to put pressure on Putilov.

Grzhebin informed me that Baron Drizen found in the exorcism of the Dybbuk in my play an analogy with the Gospel story about the banishment of demons. Thus it has become difficult to pass it. He asked me to stop by tomorrow.

There is a rumor of an abdication in the offing.

OCTOBER 1

I went with Naidich to the Department of Public Affairs. Putilov reiterated to him that we have to now wait for a reply from the Department of Police, while adding that the Jewish representatives to the ministries—Baron Gintsburg, Sliozberg, and Varshavskii—are hardly representative. And he characterized all three of them in an unflattering light.

I met with "Mitka" Rubinshtein[70] at the European Hotel. I don't know why, but in his typically fussy and pedantic way he informed me that he owns a majority of shares of the *New Times*[71] and can now call the shots at that paper.

≈

I went to see L. M. Kliachko (Lvov),[72] to ask him to intervene to speed the movement of my case through the Department of Police. It turned out he had a reception room, like some sort of minister, with dozens of people waiting in line, all of them in regard to Jewish matters. And he helps many people completely free of charge.

He promised to speak with Beletskii, the former Deputy of Police.[73]

≈

I visited F. K. Sologub. He and Anastasia Chebotarevskaia were complaining about Gorky and Pozner—that the two of them, without asking Sologub, rejected an essay that Sologub had commissioned by Berdiaev[74] for *The Shield*,[75] which is being published under the editorship of Andreev, Gorky, and Sologub. By having done so they placed Sologub in a ridiculous situation. In general he thinks he is being poorly treated.

Sologub was very upset by a simply absurd remark that appeared in *Speech* a few months ago, that "Sologub is known to be a vicious antisemite." It's true that the editorial board later issued some kind of proviso, a correction, but it wasn't enough. Sologub wrote Gessen[76] a harsh letter in which he demanded an explanation: on what basis was he calling him an antisemite, and in which of his works had Gessen found an expression of antisemitism? Gessen haughtily replied that the business of a newspaper is to serve the public, and there is no accounting for personal pride. Sologub was called an antisemite on the basis of a personal conversation that Gessen had with a man whom the editorial board completely trusts.

Sologub is certain that this person whom the editors trust is Filosofov.[77] Sologub discussed the Jewish Question only once with him and Merezhkovskii,[78] at the time when he invited them both to join the league for the defense of Jews. A number of antisemitic statements were made, but it was Merezhkovskii who had made them, not Sologub. Filosofov confused the two of them on account of his friendship with Merezhkovskii.

A. N. Chebotarevskaia described her meeting with Rasputin. She and one other person went to see the sculptor Aronson,[79] who is working on a bust of Rasputin, in order to meet Rasputin there and discuss Jewish matters with him. He greeted them rather coldly, almost antagonistically, suspecting them as rivals. Let no one interfere, he will do it all himself. He's a friend of the Jews, and the Jews themselves should turn to him. Rights? He'll secure every right for them. He obtained amnesty for the Deists, after all!

Then he entered into some kind of bizarre, sexual arousal (according to Chebotarevskaia) and began to dance. He danced for a whole hour, "and as I watched him dancing in some sort of ecstatic state in that setting," she said, "I was reminded of a scene from *The Petty Demon*."[80]

Chebotarevskaia said she wrote a play during a trip along the Volga, but because she isn't known as a writer, Sologub, who had had a hand in it here and there, signed his name to it.

I told them that I made several changes to my play according to Sulerzhitskii's recommendations: Among other things, I made the scene of the trial with the corpse more realistic. The dead man does not speak from behind a curtain; rather, the rabbi transmits his words. Sologub reacted very negatively to this revision, saying that I was mistaken in doing this, that I had ruined this part.

I told Sologub about my plans, about the Legions. He didn't express sympathy for this. Jews ought to become Russian citizens and integrate with Russians. In passing, he raised the question: "If the Jews get Palestine, what will become of the Christian holy sites?"

We spoke about the war. Citing from what officers had said, Chebotarevskaia recounted how the commandant in Kovno got so shaken up during the bombing of the fort that he flew off in an airplane. Later, when he had gotten ahold of himself, he returned in a car, but after seeing him flee, the generals had surrendered the fort. He remains in a town nearby and is awaiting trial.

The commandant in Novogeorgievsk drove a car over to a German position and brought them Russian documents and maps; thus they knew beforehand where to shoot. The maps indicated exactly where the concrete reinforcements were and where they were not. And the Germans aimed for the latter.

They also discussed the doings of the minister of Internal Affairs, Khvostov. After meeting with representatives of the press, he went to see all the journalists and left calling cards for them. This kind of attention to the press on the part of a minister is unprecedented.

≈

I stopped by the editorial office of *Russian Riches*[81] for a four-part *jour fixe*.[82]

Rusanov[83] said that in a village he visited over the summer the peasants were enigmatically discussing military defeats. When he asked them what they were talking about, they replied:

"Have you been to Torzhok?"

"No, I haven't."

"Well now, go there and have a look, and then you'll be talking."

"And what will I see?"

"You'll see exactly what our people saw. There's a pole in the town square, and there are thirteen generals strung up on thirteen chains hanging from that pole. Every one of them has a little sign pinned to his chest that says 'Spit but don't hit!' This is all for treason."

Kondrushkin[84] said the same legend was going around in Tomsk with one variation: on the boards it says, "Do not surrender honor."

Following Nikolai Nikolaevich's departure and transfer to the Caucasian Front, nothing was heard of him, and Vorontsov-Dashkov[85] continued to govern the territories. A rumor arose on that basis that N. N. had been killed.

There are stories about the reasons for Dzhunkovskii's[86] dismissal. Rasputin was swaggering about in some place, either boasting or dictating an obscene telegram to one of his cronies. Dzhunkovskii informed about this . . . and fell from grace.

≈

Peshekhonov told me that the affair with the coalition newspaper has been settled and is getting organized. For the time being, they have 100,000 rubles and are hoping to get 500,000 rubles for it.

In the evening, when I told S. Gurev about this, he said, "If such an amount does appear, there is no doubt it will be delivered by an agent provocateur. Just like it was with the earlier publication."

OCTOBER 2

My nephew Ilia arrived from the front. He is working for the Maria Pav-lovna detachment as a first-class feldsher. They are pleased with him. As with other Jews who are working at the front, he couldn't say much about Jews—he had walked past a few of them. I scolded him and sug-gested he enter into a relationship with the Relief Committee and take on some kind of duties to provide aid to the Jewish population in any locations through which his detachment passes. He agreed and I put him in touch with Kreinin.

Khurgin sent me a telegram that in accordance with my instructions he gave 200 rubles for Galicia to his brother-in-law, Dr. Blokh.

≈

Sofia Sergeevna Gurevich was here visiting from Smolensk to acquire documents. She says the circulation of the local *Herald* has greatly ex-panded. There are many refugees in the city.

≈

I went to the Central Administration for Dramatic Publishing, to see Comrade Director Baron Drizen, to whom Grzhebin had given my play for censorship. Drizen is a gentleman: very elegant, courteous, has an easy air about himself. Apparently he is a literary man, pub-lishes some historical journal, and in his past founded the "Old The-ater."[87] He informed me that he is unable to pass my play because the scene of the banishment of the Dybbuk reminds him of the Gospel parable about the banishment of the demons. However much I sought to prove to him that the Dybbuk is not a demon, and that the analogy is remote, he wouldn't budge. Finally, he went with me and the play to the director, Prince Urusov, to whom he stated his opinions. Urusov noted that in general, he does not like to seek out analogies, but without knowing the play cannot say anything. He promised to read it.

I went to see M. Gorky. There was a meeting held about the "Jewish Anthology," which I had declined to edit on account of my departure to Galicia. I offered to delegate this task to Tsinberg. Tsinberg, Vinaver, Pozner, and I were there. We came to the same decision that we had adopted beforehand.

Gorky was saying that there has been a split among workers between national-revolutionaries and internationalists.

There is a story that either Goremykin or Khvostov threatened that if the bloc[88] demands the creation of a Ministry of Public Confidence, he and the parliamentary tribunal will publish certain documents that will bring several prominent representatives of the Unions of Towns and Zemstvos into disrepute as bribe-takers. There was a wave of unrest in Moscow after their delegation was refused a reception. The crowd swarmed to Chelnokov's office but then settled down.

There are rumors that Sazonov and Bark[89] are about to resign.

I proposed the idea of publishing a pamphlet about the heroic acts of various army units to Gorky. He took an interest in this.

They say seventh- and eighth-grade gymnasium students will be taken and transferred to a school for ensign officers.

OCTOBER 3

There was a meeting of the People's Group.[90] It has hardly convened over the course of the war and is gathering now only so as to elect delegates to the Political Bureau plenum. This bothered me and I stated my views about it rather severely. It is inadmissible for the group to limit its activities to sending delegates to the plenum. Kreinin promised to convene a meeting in the next few days to consider the question of the group's activities.

OCTOBER 4

I visited Dr. Tuvim. People there were talking about the ministers, and one person claimed that several of them are of Jewish descent. Both Khvostovs[91] have a grandmother who is a Portuguese Jew, Krivoshein[92] is the son of the cantonist Krivoshei, and there was someone else. Apparently Koni[93] is also descended from Jews—a Cohen.

There is a tram strike in Moscow.

OCTOBER 5

My nephew Ilia went to see Kreinin and received instructions for distributing aid and 1,000 rubles from him.

Spent the evening at Jabotinskaia's.[94] I read my play at her house in the presence of friends. It seems they liked it. A. R. Kugel[95] said he thinks it isn't suitable for the stage. It's a literary, not a theatrical work.

OCTOBER 6

I went to see Aizenberg. He too says that in my case everything depends on Beletskii, and we will have to wait until he joins as an acting comrade in the Ministry of Interior Affairs and takes a look at my request.

My partners from the expedition, Rekhtman[96] and Iudovin,[97] have decided to head to Harbin to seek their fortunes.

OCTOBER 7

Our close circle held a gathering. We spoke about the legions, of course; people objected to them, although not in principle. SG[98] declared himself a supporter of the legions. We shared gossip. They say Minister of Justice Khvostov will be named as prime minister. They say the High Command (Ruzskii) issued an order to expel all Jews from Ostrov and Pskov provinces, but because this would have caused a great disturbance, the order was rescinded. They say Alekseev[99] has promised there will be no further expulsions.

There are now as many as eight hundred thousand refugees on the road. In many locations, this hungry and bitter army is engaged in looting.

The commandant in Kovno was sentenced to fifteen years in a labor camp. They say he is an unbelievably gutless old man, and he was entrusted with a first-class fort. They say the Germans captured 1,600 of our weapons in Kovno; 1,100 in Novogeorgievsk. The majority of them were received from Japan. The Germans have a joke about this: "Japanese weapons are delivered to Germany by way of Russia."

In wartime Germany, there have been ten times as many books published as in Allied countries.

We spoke in passing about Sologub. Gornfeld portrayed Chebotarevskaia very harshly. She used to host erotic evenings, and now she hosts Jewish ones. "She's jealous of Sologub's genius and has degraded his demeanor and works."

OCTOBER 8

Was at Baron Drizen's. He declared for the second time that he could not pass the play in this form and proposed that I rework it in this regard. How? Banish the banishment of the spirit? The play would then be destroyed. I will try on my end "to banish the spirit," and insert the words "soul," "man's shadow," etc., in its place.

≈

Minister of Internal Affairs Khovstov declared that he is prepared to grant nearly every right to the Jews, with the condition that they commit to eliminating the inflation crisis. They say Khvostov summoned Baron Gintsburg and M. A. Varshavskii in regard to this matter. What is this? A sinister joke or idiocy?

The plenum held a meeting. The whole plenum is still preoccupied with the Political Bureau's elections and chairman. It's pitifully stewing in the juices of its own politicking. In the middle of the meeting, a pale and agitated L. M. Bramson showed up and asked for the floor. The sight of him alone frightened several of us. We were certain that he had brought some kind of devastating news. We were seized by an even worse fear when he nervously choked up, began to speak in a sinister voice, and said that an event of enormous, disturbing importance had taken place that could constitute a turning point in the history of Russian Jewry.

"What is the matter? Speak!," fearful voices rang out.

This is actually what it was: lately the Relief Committee has been playing an important role in Jewish life and is becoming the most significant organ of political life. It is the local millionaires who play the leading roles on the committee's executive. It is crucial to introduce social elements to the executive. There were discussions held about this. And here today the Relief Committee's executive decided that the Petersburg Community alone possesses the decisive voice in the matter of reorganizing the executive—that is, that same handful of plutocrats. And Bramson came running here in a half-faint to the plenum, crying, "the fatherland is in danger!"

I felt at one and the same time like spitting from indignation and bursting into laughter. How is it that this man, who is so innately honest and restrained, had so vividly uttered this bureaucratic nonsense?

Earlier in the meeting I had asked to say a word and wanted to talk about the character of the plenum's activities. But with his hysterics Bramson created an atmosphere that didn't suit my speech. However, I did say a few words. I pointed out that the Political Bureau, which has consumed the entire Jewish intelligentsia in Petrograd, is controlling the political fate of the Jewish people while sitting in an office. To understand what is going on with Jewry, and the kind of demands that the people are issuing, we ought to support the young people who are volunteering on their own to go and see what is happening with their own eyes. No one displays more dedication than the youth; their dedication even surpasses that of the organizations that distribute monetary aid. But the youth cannot and do not have authority to offer advice or issue orders; they don't have the capacity to grasp the bigger picture. And the consequence of this is that all the eyewitness accounts from the field are viewed here solely as archival material for history, as material for discussions with the ministries. And Jewish politics as a whole has become a politics of lobbying the ministries; it has fallen into a craven cycle. It is crucial that we work out a plan for opening refugee shelters, a plan for combating pogroms and rape, for forging systematic ties to public organizations, political parties, national parties, and so forth. To do this, the plenum ought to break apart into sections; in addition, its members must travel to the field.

My proposal was received sympathetically, but there was no discussion about it: there was no time, for the pots were boiling over in the kitchen behind the scenes—Vinaver or Sliozberg?

They say the following incident occurred in Smorgon during the expulsion of the population and burning of the city: a Cossack officer walked into one house and ordered the people to leave at once. The owners, two brothers, told him they couldn't leave right away because their father was sick and a stretcher was needed for him.

"Where is the sick man?" the officer asked.

They took him and showed him the sick man. He took out a revolver, shot the sick man in the head, and said, "So, now you don't have to worry about your father—you can go."

Many old and sick people were burned inside of the buildings.

≈

M. L. Trivus[100] spoke with me about the legions and proposed to write something for *Jewish Week*.[101] I told him it is only worth writing if you state your position clearly and in detail. If you start with a formula— "on the one hand it is impossible not to recognize it, but on the other hand it must be said— . . ."—then it is better not to write at all.

OCTOBER 9

Was occupied the whole day with the "banishment of the spirit" from the play.

Received an invitation to an organizational meeting for the Artists' Society,[102] at the request of the sculptor Ilia Gintsburg.[103]

≈

People keep talking about Khvostov's appeal to Gintsburg and Varshavskii. This is starting to assume a truly provocative character.

The mood in Petrograd is very tense. There is no flour, sugar, or kindling. Groups of one hundred to two hundred people stand in lines at grocery shops, hoping for a turn to get a pound or two of sugar. The possibility of hunger strikes is to be feared. And at such a time, an appeal to representatives of the Jewish community with a proposal that they take it upon themselves to end the crisis is tantamount to telling the mob that Jews are the culprits behind the crisis, and heaping responsibility for it on them. And what is frightening is that Baron Gintsburg and Varshavskii find it possible to speak with the ministers about this matter, rather than simply refusing to enter into any kind of discussions.

≈

Jabotinskaia informed me that Patterson[104] appealed to Vladimir Evgenievich Jabotinsky with a proposal to send one thousand Jewish soldiers to the Dardanelles,[105] and that Trumpeldor[106] recruited one hundred soldiers in Alexandria.

In general, the situation is growing very gloomy. The whole picture will change with Bulgaria's entry into the war. England is proposing to give Cyprus to Greece[107] and is hardly likely to pursue Palestine now.

≈

People say that Lutsk was completely destroyed at the time it changed hands.

Saw Dr. Beinis from Vitebsk. He worked for a year at the front under enemy fire, was awarded with honors. Now there has been some sort of denunciation of him, and he is being transferred to Samarkand.

He described the inconceivable thefts that the Cossacks carry out. In several places, Cossacks were hanged for marauding. But this didn't help.

OCTOBER 10

Baron Drizen was satisfied with my revision of the play, the substitution of the word "spirit" with the words "soul" or "shadow"; he also asked for an angel to be banished in one place ("Tsadik of Tartakov, I know that you are commanded by angels!"), and passed the play.

≈

At night I went M. I. Sheftel's[108] house for an organizational meeting for the Artists' Society. I. I. Gintsburg, Baron Gintsburg, Maimon,[109] Aronson, M. G. Syrkin,[110] and two or three other people were there. I got the impression that Gintsburg's whole mission is to find patrons for indigent artists. I therefore proposed a mission: the nationalization of Jewish artists. The baron, Syrkin, and Gintsburg argued with this, pointing out that it isn't possible to force subjects upon artists, that art is free. I know this as well as they do, but kept trying to prove that the goal of the society is to offer artists a national milieu, to interest them in Jewry so that they develop an aspiration to work in a national vein. Until now Gintsburg, Aronson, and Pasternak haven't produced a single Jewish work.

≈

After that meeting, I went to Sologub's for a reading of his and Anastasia Chebotarevskaia's play *A Stone Cast into Water*[111] (likely hers, with his signature). I arrived late and missed the first two acts.

Notes

INTRODUCTION

1. In Russian, EKOPO stood for *Evreiskii komitet dlia pomoshchi zhertvam voiny*.

2. The point here concerns diaries only and not memoirs or retrospective accounts. While several of An-sky's notable Russian Jewish contemporaries did keep diaries about the war, none of them traveled to the front or did aid work in war zones. See, for example, Semen Dubnov, *Kniga zhizni: Vospominaniia i razmyshleniia: Materialy dlia istorii moego vremeni*, ed. Viktor Kel'ner (Saint Petersburg: Peterburgskoe vostokovedenie, 1998) (forthcoming in an English translation edited by Kel'ner and Benjamin Nathans); G. B. Sliozberg, *Dela minuvshikh dnei: Zapiski russkogo evreia*, vol. 3 (Paris: Pascal, 1933–1934); M. M. Vinaver, *Nedavnee. Vospominaniia i kharakteristiki* (Petrograd, 1917).

3. This literature, in multiple languages, is too vast to summarize here, but among notable recent publications in English that include eyewitness accounts of Russia's war, see Peter Englund, *The Beauty and the Sorrow: An Intimate History of the First World War* (New York: Vintage Books, 2011). Many previously unpublished personal accounts are described in Joshua A. Sanborn, *Imperial Apocalypse: The Great War and the Destruction of the Russian Empire* (New York: Oxford University Press, 2014). A guide to English-language personal accounts of the war is Edward Lengel, *World War I Memories: An Annotated Bibliography of Personal Accounts Published in English since 1919* (Lanham, MD: Scarecrow Press, 2004). In Russian, a catalogue of diaries and memoirs written during the war can be found in the fourth volume of the bibliographic guide *Istoriia Dorevoliutsionnoi Rossii v dnevnikakh i vospominaniiakh 1895–1917*, 4 vols. (Moscow: Kniga, 1983).

4. On the origins of the Pale of Settlement, see John Klier, *Russia Gathers Her Jews: The Origins of the 'Jewish Question' in Russia, 1772–1825* (DeKalb: Northern Illinois University Press, 1986).

5. Scholars have noted that it is easier to describe than to define a shtetl, which had no fixed size, but did have a typical social geography that was centered around the town square (*rynek*) where the weekly market took place. In John Klier's

formulation, the average shtetl operated as the "centre of an economic-cultural zone, linking Jews to Christians and Jews to Jews" ("What Exactly Was a Shtetl?" in *The Shtetl: Image and Reality*, ed. Gennady Estraikh and Mikhail Krutikov [Oxford: Legenda Books, 2000], 23–35, here 26). For a historical survey of the shtetl in its Russian imperial context, see Ben-Cion Pinchuk, "The Shtetl: An Ethnic Town in the Russian Empire," *Cahiers du Monde Russe* 41, no. 4 (2000): 495–504.

6. S. An-sky, foreword to *The Jewish Ethnographic Program*, trans. Nathaniel Deutsch, in Deutsch, *The Jewish Dark Continent: Life and Death in the Russian Pale of Settlement* (Cambridge: Harvard University Press, 2011), 103–104.

7. See Irina Paperno, *Stories of the Soviet Experience: Memoirs, Diaries, Dreams* (Ithaca, NY: Cornell University Press, 2009); Jane Gary Harris, "Diversity of Discourse: Autobiographical Statements in Theory and Praxis," in *Autobiographical Statements in Twentieth Century Russian Literature*, ed. Jane G. Harris (Princeton: Princeton University Press, 1990), 3–35.

8. I. L. Peretz, Yankev Dinezon, and S. An-sky-Rappoport, "Oyfruf," *Haynt*, no. 292, December 19, 1914/January 1, 1915, 3; translation published as "Appeal to Collect Materials about the World War," trans. David G. Roskies, in *The Literature of Destruction: Jewish Responses to Catastrophe*, ed. Roskies (New York: Jewish Publication Society, 1988), 209–210.

9. On the original number of documents and objects, see F. Shargorodskaia, "O nasledii An-skogo," *Evreiskaia Starina* no. 11 (1924): 309. The remnants of An-sky's war archive are at the Jewish Manuscript Division of the Vernadsky National Library of Ukraine in Kiev (*Natsional'naia Biblioteka Ukraini imeni Vernadskogo*, or NBUV). The bibliography of NBUV's An-sky holdings has been published: see Irina Sergeeva, *Arkhivna spadshchina Semena An-s'kogo* (Kyiv: Dukh i litera, 2006).

10. For the Historical-Ethnographic Society's appeal, see "Arkhiv i Muzei Evreiskago Istoriko-etnograficheskago Obshchestva," *Evreiskaia starina* no. 8 (1915): 428. On the volumes collected by the Russian Jewish political leadership, see my essay "Reconstructing a Lost Archive: Simon Dubnow and 'The Black Book of Imperial Russian Jewry.' Materials for a History of the War, 1914–1915," *Simon Dubnow Institute Yearbook* 12 (2013): 419–442, at 436.

11. The literary origins of Jewish autobiographical texts are described in Marcus Moseley, *Being for Myself Alone: Origins of Jewish Autobiography* (Stanford: Stanford University Press, 2006). Although Moseley considers only Hebrew and non-Hebrew or Yiddish texts in his analysis of Jewish autobiographical literature, some of his findings do apply to An-sky's Russian war diary. In Dubnov's diary, for example (which the author originally wrote in Russian but later published in Hebrew and Yiddish translations), Moseley (458) suggests a confluence of the "historical, the ideological and the autobiographical" modes of thought.

12. Gabriella Safran, *Wandering Soul: S. An-sky, Creator of the Dybbuk* (Cambridge: Harvard University Press, 2010), 280–281.

13. Rossiiskii Gosudarstvennyi Arkhiv Literatury i Iskusstva (Russian State Archive of Literature and Art, or RGALI). S. An-skii, diary for January 1–March 8,

1915, at fond 2583, opis' 1, delo 5, ll. 3–63; diary for September 9–October 10, 1915, at fond 2583, opis' 1, delo 5, ll. 21–40. Gabriella Safran (*Wandering Soul*, 339n51) writes that "the absence of later diaries [at RGALI] suggests they were sent to Vilna," although physical copies of them have not surfaced to date.

14. Letter from An-sky to H. N. Bialik of April 23, 1918, cited in Safran, *Wandering Soul*, 280.

15. In Yiddish, Sh. An-ski, *Der Yudisher Khurbn fun poylen galitsye un bukovina, fun tog-bukh 1914–1917*, in *Gezamelte shriftn in fuftsen bender*, vols. 4–6 (Vilna, Poland: Farlag "An-sky," 1921–1928).

16. S. An-ski, *Hurban ha-Yehudim be-Polin, Galitsyah u-Bukovinah*, trans. S. L. Tsitron (Berlin: A. Y. Stybel, 1929).

17. The most complete, although still abridged translation is S. Ansky, *The Enemy at His Pleasure: A Journey through the Jewish Pale of Settlement during World War I*, trans. and ed. Joachim Neugroschel (New York: Metropolitan Books, 2002). A forty-page English-language excerpt appeared as *The Destruction of Galicia: Excerpts from a Diary, 1914–1917*, in S. Ansky, *The Dybbuk and Other Writings*, ed. David G. Roskies, trans. Golda Werman (New Haven: Yale University Press, 2002), 169–208.

18. The definitive biography of An-sky is Safran, *Wandering Soul*; see also the collection of essays in *The Worlds of S. An-sky: A Russian-Jewish Intellectual at the Turn of the Century*, ed. Gabriella Safran and Steven Zipperstein (Stanford: Stanford University Press, 2006); as well as the translation of An-sky's first Russian novella, *Pioneers: A Tale of Russian-Jewish Life in the 1880s*, trans. Michael R. Katz (Bloomington: Indiana University Press, 2014). Recent studies of the ethnographic expedition include Deutsch, *The Jewish Dark Continent*; Eugene M. Avrutin, Valerii Dymshits, Alexander Ivanov, Alexander Lvov, Harriet Murav, and Alla Sokolova, eds., *Photographing the Jewish Nation: Pictures from S. An-sky's Ethnographic Expeditions* (Waltham: Brandeis University Press, 2009); A. Kantsedikas and I. Sergeyeva, *The Jewish Artistic Heritage Album by Semyon An-sky*, trans. Ludmila Lezhneva and Alan Myers (Moscow: Mosty Kultury, 2001); Mariella Beukers and Renée Waale, eds., *Tracing An-sky: Jewish Collections from the State Ethnographic Museum in St. Petersburg* (Zwolle, Netherlands: Waanders Uitgevers/Amsterdam: Joods Historisch Museum, 1992).

19. Historical studies that cite *The Destruction of Galicia* include Peter Holquist, "The Role of Personality in the First (1914–1915) Russian Occupation of Galicia and Bukovina," in *Anti-Jewish Violence: Rethinking the Pogrom in East European History*, ed. Jonathan Dekel-Chen, David Gaunt, Natan M. Meir, and Israel Bartal (Bloomington: Indiana University Press, 2010), 52–73; Larry Wolff, *The Idea of Galicia: History and Fantasy in Habsburg Political Culture* (Stanford: Stanford University Press, 2010), 351–361; Aviel Roshwald, "Jewish Cultural Identity in Eastern and Central Europe during the Great War," in *European Culture in the Great War: The Arts, Entertainment, and Propaganda, 1914–1918*, ed. Aviel Roshwald and Richard Stites (Cambridge: Cambridge University Press, 1999), 89–126; Steven J. Zipperstein, "The Politics of Relief: The Transformation of Russian Jewish

Communal Life during the First World War," in *Studies in Contemporary Jewry IV: Jews and the European Crisis*, ed. Jonathan Frankel (Oxford: Oxford University Press, 1988), 22–40.

20. David G. Roskies was the first scholar to describe *Khurbn Galitsye* as a Jewish cultural response to a catastrophic historical event, in his *Against the Apocalypse: Responses to Catastrophe in Modern Jewish Culture* (Syracuse: Syracuse University Press, 1999); and idem., *The Jewish Search for a Usable Past* (Bloomington: Indiana University Press, 1999).

21. For a comprehensive discussion of the first year of the war in Russia, see Sanborn, *Imperial Apocalypse*, 21–64.

22. *Polozhenie o polevom upravlenii voisk v voennoe vremia* (Petrograd: Voennaia Tip. imperatritsy Ekateriny Velikoi, 1914); Daniel W. Graf, "Military Rule behind the Russian Front, 1914–1917: The Political Ramifications," *Jahrbücher für Geschichte Osteuropas* Neue Folge 22, no. 3 (1974): 390–411.

23. Population figure cited from Benjamin Nathans, *Beyond the Pale: The Jewish Encounter with Late Imperial Russia* (Berkeley: University of California Press, 2002), 92.

24. On prewar Jewish philanthropy and concepts of Jewish enlightenment, see Brian Horowitz, *Jewish Philanthropy and Enlightenment in Late-Tsarist Russia* (Seattle: University of Washington Press, 2009); Jeffrey Veidlinger, *Jewish Public Culture in Late Imperial Russia* (Bloomington: Indiana University Press, 2009), 229–291.

25. On EKOPO's history, see my essay, "Fighting 'On Our Own Territory': The Rescue and Representation of Jews in Russia during World War I," in *Russia's Home Front in War and Revolution. Book 2: The Experience of War and Revolution*, ed. Adele Lindenmeyr, Christopher Read, and Peter Waldron (Bloomington: Slavica Publishers, forthcoming); Yevgeniya Pevzner, "Jewish Committee for the Relief of War Victims (1914–1921)," *Pinkas* 1 (2006): 114–142; Simon Rabinovich, *Jewish Rights, National Rites: Nationalism and Autonomy in Late Imperial and Revolutionary Russia* (Stanford: Stanford University Press, 2014), chap. 5; A. S. Tumanova, "Evreiskie obshchestvennye organizatsii v gody Pervoi mirovoi voiny, na primere Tambovskoi gubernii" in *Mirovoi krizis*, 124–142; Zipperstein, "The Politics of Relief."

26. On spy mania in wartime Russia, see William C. Fuller Jr., *The Foe Within: Fantasies of Treason and the End of Imperial Russia* (Ithaca, NY: Cornell University Press, 2006), chap. 6.

27. Evidence of Ianushkevich's antisemitism was registered in a series of meetings held by Russian ministers from July to September 1915, transcriptions of which were later published as A. N. Iakhontov, "Tiazhelye dni: Sekretnyia zasedaniia Soveta Ministrov 16 Iulia–2 Sentiabria 1915 goda, Sostavleno A. N. Iakhontovym," *Arkhiv Russkoi revoliutsii* 18 (Berlin, 1926): 5–136, here 12, 32, 42–51, 57.

28. Eric Lohr has characterized Russian military violence during the war as "military pogroms," in "The Russian Army and the Jews: Mass Deportation,

Hostages, and Violence during World War I," *Russian Review* 60 (2001): 404–419, here at 406–407; military orders for expulsions of Jews are published in Lohr, "Novye dokumenty o Rossiiskoi Armii i evreiakh vo vremena Pervoi mirovoi voiny," *Vestnik evreiskogo universiteta* 26 (2003): 245–268. On the military pogroms, see also John Klier, "Kazaki i pogromy: Chem otlichalis' 'voennye' pogromy?" in *Mirovoi krizis 1914–1920 godov i sud'ba vostochnoevropeiskogo evreistva*, ed. O. V. Budnitskii, O. V. Belova, V. E. Kel'ner, and V. V. Mochalova (Moscow: Rosspen, 2005), 45–70.

29. In 1910, Jews numbered 871,906, or 11 percent of the total population in Galicia, and 102,919, or 13 percent of the population in Bukovina (Marsha L. Rozenblit, *Reconstructing a National Identity: The Jews of Habsburg Austria during World War I* [Oxford: Oxford University Press, 2001], 15).

30. Most of the Galician refugees streamed west to the empire's capital cities of Vienna and Cracow; a smaller number went south into Hungarian territory. See Arieh Tartakower and Kurt R. Grossman, *The Jewish Refugee* (New York: International Press, 1944), 14; Rozenblit, *Reconstructing a National Identity*, 15.

31. Nikolai Golovin, "The Great Battle of Galicia (1914): A Study in Strategy," *The Slavonic Review* 5, no. 13 (1926): 25–47, here 46.

32. The Russian-Jewish weekly *Novyi voskhod* (New Dawn), published in Petrograd at the time, reprinted accounts of the Lvov pogrom of September 27–28 that were originally printed in the liberal Russian newspaper *Novoe vremia* (*Novyi voskhod*, no. 39, October 2, 1914, 21).

33. S. An-skii, "Putevyia zametki," *Rech'*, no. 279, October 16 [29], 1914, 2.

34. S. An-skii, "V evreiskom lazarete," *Den'*, November 28, 1914, 324.

35. Safran, *Wandering Soul*, 227–228.

36. The Union of Zemstvos was known as *Vserossiskii zemskii soiuz*, or VZS. The Union of Towns was known as *Vserossiskii soiuz gorodov*, or VSG.

37. William Gleason, "The All-Russian Union of Zemstvos and World War I," in *The Zemstvo in Russia: An Experiment in Local Self-Government*, ed. Terence Emmons and Wayne S. Vucinich (Cambridge: Cambridge University Press, 1982), 365–382.

38. Peter Gatrell, *A Whole Empire Walking: Refugees in Russia during World War I* (Bloomington: Indiana University Press, 2005), 39; Heinz-Dietrich Löwe, *The Tsars and the Jews: Reform, Reaction and Anti-Semitism in Imperial Russia, 1772–1917* (Chur, Switzerland: Harwood Academic Publishers, 1993), 326–327. Throughout the first year of war, Jews made up just over 9 percent of all VSG and VZS employees on the Southwest Front—less than the percentage of Jews living in western Russia. In August 1916, then Chief of Staff Mikhail Alekseev wrote to the chairman of the Union of Zemstvos, Prince Georgii L'vov, to ask him to remove Jews working for the unions, as they were widely suspected to be dodging military service or else disseminating revolutionary propaganda.

39. Hausner's son Gideon, born in Lvov in September 1915, went on to become the attorney general in Israel who prosecuted Adolf Eichmann in 1961.

40. N. M. Gelber, ed., "Toldot Yehude Lvov," in *Entsiklopedyah shel galuyot*, vol. 4 (Jerusalem, 1956), col. 339.

41. Ibid.

42. A. Iu. Bakhturina, *Politika Rossiiskoi Imperii v Vostochnoi Galitsii v gody Pervoi mirovoi voiny* (Moscow: AIRO-XX, 2000); Mark Von Hagen, *War in a European Borderland: Occupations and Occupation Plans in Galicia and Ukraine, 1914–1918* (Seattle: University of Washington Press, 2007).

43. The population of East Galicia included 65 percent Ruthenians, 22 percent Poles, and 13 percent Jews; the West had 88 percent Poles, 4 percent Ruthenians, and 8 percent Jews (Joshua Shanes, *Diaspora Nationalism and Jewish Identity in Habsburg Galicia* [New York: Cambridge University Press, 2012], 3, 17–18).

44. Bakhturina, *Politika*, 142–143, 160, 170.

45. Patricia Herlihy, "Ukrainian Cities in the Nineteenth Century," in *Rethinking Ukrainian History*, ed. Ivan L. Rudnytsky (Edmonton: The Canadian Institute of Ukrainian Studies at The University of Alberta, 1981), 135–155, here 143–145. Herlihy notes that Lvov had fourteen Ukrainian schools in 1914.

46. Holquist, "The Role of Personality," describes plans concocted by a low-ranking Foreign Ministry official—the attaché to the Southwestern Front, Court Chamberlain V. Murav'ev—to cleanse Galicia and Bukovina of all Jews. Murav'ev traveled to Czernowitz after its occupation by Russian forces in fall 1914 and advocated a mass expulsion of Jews from Galicia. His plans received support from General Ianushkevich and the Commander in Chief Nikolai Nikolaevich but were never carried out due to the Russian withdrawal from Galicia in spring 1915. Although never carried out, Murav'ev's proposal plans gained the support of the Russian Army commander in chief and even the tsar.

47. On the Brody pogrom, see Holquist, "The Role of Personality," 54–56.

48. On the Lvov pogrom, see Alexander V. Prusin, *Nationalizing a Borderland: War, Ethnicity and Anti-Jewish Violence in East Galicia, 1914–1920* (Tuscaloosa: University of Alabama Press, 2005), 30–32.

49. On hostages, see Bakhturina, *Politika*, 193–194; on deportations of Jews, see Dubnov, ed., "Iz 'chernoi knigi' russkago evreistva, materialy dlia istorii voiny, 1914–1915," *Evreiskaia Starina* 10 (1918): 231–253.

50. Russian authorities' attempts to combat inflation are documented and discussed in Sanborn, *Imperial Apocalypse*, 43–51.

51. Gelber, ed., "Toldot Yehude Lvov," col. 338.

52. The 1907 elections are the subject of Shanes, *Diaspora Nationalism*, chap. 5.

53. Salo Wittmayer Baron, *Under Two Civilizations: Tarnow, 1895–1914* (Stanford: Stanford University Press, 1990), n.p.

54. Alison Fleig Frank, *Oil Empire: Visions of Prosperity in Austrian Galicia* (Cambridge: Harvard University Press, 2005), 126–129.

55. Figures of Jewish landowners in Galicia are cited from Tomasz Gąsowski, "From *Austeria* to the Manor: Jewish Landowners in Autonomous Galicia," in *Polin: Studies in Polish Jewry*, vol. 12, *Galicia: Jews, Poles, and Ukrainians, 1772–1918*, ed.

Israel Bartal and Antony Polonsky (1999): 120–136, here at 131–133. On Ruthenian peasants' identification of Jews with the manor, see John-Paul Himka, "Dimensions of a Triangle: Polish-Ukrainian-Jewish Relations in Austrian Galicia," in *Polin* 12: 25–48, here at 30.

56. Lohr, "The Russian Army and the Jews."

57. Bakhturina, *Politika*, 187–189.

58. The minsters' lengthy debates in meetings of August 4 and 6, 1915, concerning the expansion of the Pale are transcribed in A. N. Iakhontov, "Tiazhelye dni," 44–72, passim.

59. An-sky's life for the period described in his September and October diary entries is discussed in detail in Safran, *Wandering Soul*, 247–252.

60. On the composition and themes of *The Dybbuk*, see Safran, *Wandering Soul*, 211–222; on the Russian variant discovered in the St. Petersburg Theater Library in 2001, see Vladislav Ivanov, introduction to S. An-sky, *Between Two Worlds (The Dybbuk): Censored Variant*, trans. Anne Eakin Moss, in *Worlds of S. An-sky*, 361–373.

61. On An-sky's Zionism, see Safran, *Wandering Soul*, 251–252; Brian Horowitz, "Spiritual and Physical Strength in An-sky's Literary Imagination," in *Worlds of S. An-sky*, 103–118. On responses among Russian Zionists to Jabotinsky's ideas see Rafael' Grugman, *Vladimir Zhabotinskii: Neukrotimyi Samson* (Herzliya, Israel: Isradon, 2010), 61–78; Hillel Halkin, *Jabotinsky: A Life* (New Haven: Yale University Press, 2014), 86–111.

62. On the use of data about Jewish war victims that EKOPO relief workers gathered in the field, see my "Reconstructing a Lost Archive."

63. The documentary compilation was published in Russian as "Iz 'chernoi knigi' rossiiskago evreistva: Materialy dlia istorii voiny 1914–1915 g.," *Evreiskaia starina* no. 10 (1918): 195–296. On the letter to Dubnov, see V. E. Kel'ner, *Missioner istorii: Zhizn' i trudy Semena Markovicha Dubnova* (St. Petersburg: "Mir," 2008), 501.

64. For a discussion about An-sky's prewar views of language politics and Jewish culture, see Safran, *Wandering Soul*, chap. 7.

65. An-sky titled the Russian-language summary "Razrushenie Galitsii" (The Destruction of Galicia). For the original source, see NBUV f. 339, ed. kh. 89. It has also been published, as S. An-skii, "Razrushenie Galitsii," ed. I. A. Sergeeva, *Arkhiv Evreiskoi Istorii* (Moscow: Rosspen, 2006), 3: 18–30.

66. An-sky noted the agreement with Stybel in a letter of May 5, 1917, to his friend Roza Monoszon, published as "Pis'ma S. An-skogo," *Novyi zhurnal* 89 (1967): 115–131, here at 122; on the Hebrew translation, see An-sky's letter to H. N. Bialik of April 23, 1918, cited in Safran, *Wandering Soul*, 280.

67. A. Kahan [Abraham Cahan], "Vilne, 1919. Av. Kahan vegn zayn arest in Vilne," http://yiddish2.forward.com/node/3273 (accessed November 12, 2014). For a history of Jews in Vilna during the war see Andrew N. Koss, *World War I and the Remaking of Jewish Vilna, 1914–1918* (Ph.D. dissertation, Stanford University, 2010).

68. Jacob Wygodski, *In Shturm* (Vilna, Poland: Farlag B. Kletskin, 1926). I am grateful to Gennady Estraikh for this reference. Wygodski also recounted An-sky's

years in Vilna in a Yiddish commemorative publication issued shortly after the latter's death: Jacob Wygodski, "Sh. An-ski, Zikhroynes," *Lebn* 7-8 (Dec. 1920): 41–42. For another notable example of a Yiddish-language war memoir written by a Russian-Jewish intellectual (also mentioned by An-sky in his diary on September 13, 1915), see Shmaryahu Levin, *In milḥome-tsayṭen: Bleṭer fun a ṭoge-bukh*, 2 vols. (New York: American Zionist Federation, 1915–1917).

69. *Vilner zamlbukh*, ed. Tsemakh Shabad and Moshe Shalit, 2 vols. (Vilna, Germany: 1918). On this effort, see Samuel Kassow, "Jewish Communal Politics in Transition: The Vilna Kehile, 1919–1920," in *YIVO Annual*, vol. 20, ed. Deborah Dash Moore (Evanston, IL, and New York: Northwestern University Press and the YIVO Institute for Jewish Research, 1991), 61–91.

70. On An-sky's efforts in Vilna in the immediate postwar period, see Safran, *Wandering Soul*, 282; Cecile E. Kuznitz, "An-sky's Legacy: the Vilna Historic-Ethnographic Society and the Shaping of Modern Jewish Culture," in *The Worlds of S. An-sky*, 320–345; and idem., *YIVO and the Making of Modern Jewish Culture: Scholarship for the Yiddish Nation* (New York: Cambridge University Press, 2014), 24–30.

71. S. An-sky letter to Chaim Zhitlowsky, October 11, 1920, cited in Safran, *Wandering Soul*, 287.

72. Abraham G. Duker, *Jews in World War I: A Brief Historical Sketch* (New York: The American Jewish Committee, 1939), 8.

73. Herman Kruk, *The Last Days of the Jerusalem of Lithuania: Chronicles from the Vilna Ghetto and the Camps, 1939–1944*, ed. Benjamin Harshav, trans. Barbara Harshav (London and New York: Yale University Press and the YIVO Institute for Jewish Research, 2002), 475.

74. For a comprehensive discussion and excerpts of the vast memorial book literature, see *From a Ruined Garden: The Memorial Books of Polish Jewry*, ed. and trans. Jack Kugelmass and Jonathan Boyarin (Bloomington: Indiana University Press, 1998). The following memorial books include excerpts in Hebrew or Yiddish from *The Destruction of Galicia*: Sh. An-ski, "Zholkiv b'eyney sofer," Sefer Zholkiv [Żółkiew] (Jerusalem: Entsiklopediah shel galuyot, 1969), 299–302 [Hebrew]; Sh. An-ski, "Reysho b'milkhamah ha'olam ha'rishonah 1914–1918," in *Kehilat Reysho* [Rzeszów] (Tel Aviv: Former Residents of Rzeszow in Israel and the USA, 1967), 238 [Hebrew]; Sh. An-ski, "Eyn Khorostkov bet der ershter velt-milkhomeh," in *Sefer Khorotskov* (Tel Aviv: "Orli," 1968), 258–263 [Yiddish; in English, see S. Ansky, "In Khorostkov during the First World War," in *From a Ruined Garden*, 179–182].

1. WINTER 1915

1. Rovno (Ukrainian, Rivne; Polish, Równe): 1897 population: 19,737 (Jewish population: 13,462, or 68.2%); 1921 population: 30,482 (Jewish population: 21,702, or 71.2%). These and all subsequent population figures cited from Bohdan

Wasiutyński, *Ludność żydowska w Polsce w wiekach XIX i XX* (Warsaw: Instytut popierania nauki, 1930).

2. German, a lot of onion.

3. Yitzhak Asher Naidich (1868–1949), Russian-Jewish industrialist, Zionist activist, patron, and member of Moscow branch of the Jewish Committee for the Aid of War Victims (EKOPO).

4. Part of Russian Army's Northwest Front with Germany, which stretched from the Baltic Sea to central Poland.

5. According to the Julian calendar (used in the Russian Empire until January 1918), German troops would have celebrated the new year on December 19, 1914.

6. Grand Duke Nikolai Nikolaevich (1856–1929), Supreme Commander in Chief of the Russian Army (August 1914–August 1915), and first cousin once removed, of Tsar Nicholas II.

7. Paul von (Pavel Karlovich) Rennenkampf (1854–1918), Russian general, commander of the First Army (July 1914–November 1914). He was widely suspected of treason due to military incompetence on the battlefield and suspicions about his German origins.

8. Igor Platonovich Demidov (1873–1946), Russian liberal aristocrat, zemstvo activist, and a Kadet Party deputy to the Fourth Duma.

9. Lev Platonovich Demidov (1870–1919), Russia liberal aristocrat, and zemstvo activist.

10. Boris Efimovich Ratner (1883–1961), Russian-Jewish socialist lawyer from Moscow.

11. Russian, a collective of workers who hired themselves out to an employer.

12. Refers to the Jewish Committee to Aid War Victims (Russian, *Evreiskii komitet dlia pomoshchi zhertvam voiny*, or EKOPO), the organization that hired An-sky to aid Jewish war victims in Russian-occupied Galicia in November 1914.

13. Nikolai Aleksandrovich Popov (1871–1949), Russian theater director and playwright; member of the Society of Art and Literature and close friend of Konstantin Stanislavskii (1863–1938), head of the Moscow Art Theater.

14. Vladimir Ivanovich Nemirovich-Danchenko (1858–1943), Russian playwright, theater director, and cofounder of the Moscow Art Theater in 1898.

15. Refers to An-sky's Russian-language play *Between Two Worlds* (*The Dybbuk*).

16. Leontii Moiseevich Bramson (1869–1941), Russian-Jewish historian, liberal politician, and secretary of EKOPO during the war.

17. Aleksandr Isaevich Braudo (1888–1945), Russian-Jewish historian and activist, director of Imperial Public Library in St. Petersburg, and patron of Jewish culture.

18. Iosif Menassievich Bikerman (1867–1942), Russian-Jewish historian, publicist, journalist, and liberal political leader.

19. Solomon Vladimirovich Pozner (1880–1945), Russian-Jewish lawyer, historian, and publicist.

20. Refers to The Russian Society for the Study of Jewish Life (*Ruskago Obshchestva dlia izucheniia evreiskoi zhizni*), founded in December 1914 in Petrograd by the writers Maksim Gorky, Fyodor Sologub, and Leonid Andreev.

21. Maksim Gorky (Aleksei Maksimovich Peshkov) (1868–1936), Russian author and publicist, Social Democratic revolutionary, known for founding the Socialist realist literary method in Soviet times.

22. Leonid Nikolaevich Andreev (1871–1919), Russian Silver Age playwright, novelist, and short story writer.

23. Fyodor Kuzmich Sologub (1863–1927), Russian Silver Age symbolist poet, essayist, and playwright.

24. Russian, *Den'*. Russian daily liberal newspaper published in St. Petersburg.

25. Refers to the museum attached to the Jewish Historical-Ethnographic Society (*Evreiskoe istoriko-etnograficheskoe obshchestvo*), founded in 1908 in St. Petersburg.

26. Genrikh Borisovich Sliozberg (1863–1937), leading Russian-Jewish lawyer, member of St. Petersburg's Jewish Community Executive, and EKOPO's director during the war.

27. Maksim Moiseevich Vinaver (1862 or 1863–1926), leading Russian-Jewish lawyer, historian, cultural worker, and liberal politician.

28. Izrail Anshelovich Rozov (1869–1948), Russian-Jewish industrialist, Zionist publicist, founder in 1907 of the Russian-language Zionist weekly paper *Rassvet* (Dawn) in St. Petersburg.

29. Avram Davidovich Idelson (1865–1921), Russian-Jewish writer, Zionist publicist, theorist, and author.

30. Refers to the Ottoman Empire's cancellation of the Capitulations, a centuries-old system of privileges that allowed foreign subjects, including Russian and French subjects, to reside and work in Ottoman territory under the protection of their home consuls.

31. This likely refers to the EKOPO division in Moscow.

32. Georgii Sergeevich Burdzhalov (1869–1924), Russian actor and playwright, cofounder of the Moscow Art Theater.

33. Pseudonym of Ivan Vasilievich Ivanov (1867–1920), Russian theater critic.

34. Sergei Pavlovich Ordynskii (1870–1929), Russian lawyer, historian, and journalist.

35. Refers to the German howitzer, or what the Allies called "Big Bertha."

36. Evgenii Adolfovich Ganeizer (1861–1938), Polish prose writer, translator, publicist, and war correspondent.

37. Russian, *Russkie vedomosti*. Liberal daily paper published in Moscow since 1863.

38. Russian, *Utro Rossii*. Conservative Russian daily published in Moscow since 1907; it was the only Russian paper to employ war correspondents on both the Eastern and Western Fronts, and it published special editions on the war.

39. Russian, *Golos Moskvy*. An Octobrist Party organ published in Moscow since 1906.

40. Russian, *Vserossiiskii Soiuz Gorodov*, official public organization authorized by the Russian government to aid military and civilian populations in the empire's cities and towns.

41. A small town about two hundred miles northeast of Kiev.

42. Moisei Saveliev Mazor, Russian-Jewish lawyer in Kiev; former member of the Kiev committee branch of An-sky's pre-war ethnographic expedition.

43. I. M. Makhover, Zionist activist and secretary to Baron Vladimir Goratsievich Gintsburg (see n. 48).

44. Naum Solomonovich Syrkin (1878–1918), Zionist writer and publicist; former member of the Kiev committee branch of An-sky's pre-war ethnographic expedition.

45. Grigorii Borisovich Bykhovskii (1861–1936), prominent Russian-Jewish surgeon and philanthropist in Kiev; former member of the Kiev committee branch of An-sky's pre-war ethnographic expedition.

46. Iulii Grigorievich Gepner (?–1938), Russian-Jewish industrialist and owner of large sugar factory in Kiev; former member of the Kiev committee branch of An-sky's pre-war ethnographic expedition.

47. The pood was part of the old Russian system of measurement, equivalent to 36.11 pounds; 750 pood are equivalent to about 26,000 pounds.

48. Baron Vladimir Goratsievich Gintsburg (1873–1932), Russian-Jewish banking magnate and son of Baron Goratsii Evzelevich Gintsburg (1833–1909); he was An-sky's most important patron during the prewar ethnographic expedition.

49. Radivilov (Ukrainian, Radyvyliv; Polish, Radziwiłłów): 1897 population: 7,325 (Jewish population: 4,322, or 59%); 1921 population: 4,240 (Jewish population: 2,036, or 48%).

50. Moisei Akimovich Ginzburg (born Moshe Mendel Mess) (1851–1936), Russian-Jewish industrialist and patron; he was the main sponsor of the museum attached to the Jewish Historical-Ethnograpic Museum where An-sky stored objects from the Ethnographic Expedition.

51. Khlestakov refers to the main character in Nikolai Gogol's 1836 play *The Government Inspector*, an arrogant and dimwitted civil servant from St. Petersburg who impersonates a government inspector in a small Russian town.

52. The gender of the Russian noun for war, *voina*, is feminine.

53. Brody: 1910 population: 18,055 (Jewish population: 12,138, or 67.5%); 1921 population: 10,083 (Jewish population: 7,202, or 66.3%).

54. Unit of measurement used in Imperial Russia; a verst is equivalent to one kilometer, or 0.663 miles. Seven or eight versts is about five miles.

55. Łomża is about 145 kilometers (90 miles) northeast of Warsaw; at this time, it was part of the Russian Army's Northwest Front.

56. Refers to Franz Joseph (1830–1916), emperor of Austria (1848–1916) and king of Hungary (1867–1916). "Osipovich" is a play on the Russian patronymic form of Josef.

57. Seven or eight degrees below zero is about eighteen degrees Fahrenheit.

58. Polish, "Esteemed sir, please, some coal."

59. Yiddish, time of year; in Judaism, the anniversary observed for the death of a parent, spouse, sibling, or child.

60. According to Jewish law, a minimum of ten men (in Hebrew, a minyan, or quorum) must be present in order to recite the mourners' prayer (Kaddish) in public.

61. The first day of every month in the Hebrew calendar is marked by the appearance of a new moon, over which special blessings are recited during prayer services.

62. David Fadeevich Fainberg (1840–1916), prominent Russian-Jewish lawyer and public activist.

63. Georgii Aleksandrovich Bobrinskii (1863–1928), Russian governor-general of Galicia (1914–1915).

64. Wild Division (Russian, *Dikaia diviziia*) was formally known as the Caucasian Native Cavalry and consisted of Russian officers who commanded Muslim recruits (commonly confused with, but different from, Cossack troops).

65. Turkish, an expression, literally, "hack off the head" or decapitate.

66. Yiddish, side locks of hair, typically worn by Hasidic men.

67. A Moscow restaurant renowned for its interior artwork and as a meeting place for intellectuals and artists.

68. Russian, *Dvorianskaia Organizatsiia*, an association for local self-government led by nobles.

69. Dates are given according to the Gregorian calendar.

70. Hebrew, free primary school for Jewish children supported by community funds.

71. Hebrew, a charity for indigent people (literally, "bread for the poor").

72. Hebrew, executive body that oversaw the local Jewish population's internal life and external relations, including the distribution of funds for public institutions.

73. An-sky was probably referring to the Gentry Organization here.

74. Evlogii Georgievskii (1868–1946), Archbishop of Russian-occupied Galicia during the war, tasked with promoting conversion of the Ruthenian population to Russian Orthodoxy.

75. Turkish, head or chief of a Cossack military unit.

76. Lvov (Ukrainian, Lviv; Polish, Lwów; German, Lemberg): 1910 population: 206,113 (Jewish population: 57,387, or 27.8%); 1921 population: 219,388 (Jewish population: 76,854, or 35%).

77. Herman (Yankev) Diamand (1860–1931), Polish-Jewish lawyer, publisher; Lemberg representative of the Polish Social Democratic Party to the Austrian Parliament (1907–1911).

78. Fridel Evseevich Lander (1878?–193?), Russian-Jewish military doctor and Socialist Revolutionary activist; during the war, he worked for the Kiev division of the Jewish Committee for the Relief of War Victims.

79. Tsemakh Shabad (1864–1935), Russian-Jewish physician, politician, and community activist from Vilna; a close friend of An-sky's.

80. Sergei Vladimirovich Sheremetev (1880–1968), Russian military governor of Lvov (September 3–18, 1914); scion of an influential Russian noble family.

81. Major-General Eikhe's title was mayor-commandant (*gradonachal'nik*) of Lvov (September 1914–June 1915).

82. Yom Kippur: Hebrew, Day of Atonement, laws of which include fasting and other abstentions; the liturgy for Yom Kippur contains requests that God forgive personal sins. The pogrom in Lvov took place September 27–28, 1914.

83. An estimated twenty to fifty Jews were killed during the Lvov pogrom.

84. Hebrew, all vows; the first order of prayers recited after Yom Kippur begins at sundown.

85. Lvov's total population in 1914 was estimated at 212,030 residents.

86. *Gemina* is the Polish equivalent for the Hebrew word *kahal*, or executive council of the Jewish community.

87. German, secondary school system lower in rank than the gymnasium; a German model adopted throughout Europe.

88. After 1867, Emperor Franz Joseph agreed to a dualist Austro-Hungarian Empire and a constitution that granted Poles autonomy to administer institutions of municipal and provincial government in Galicia.

89. The subject was likely to have been Abraham Kohn (1807–1848), Reform rabbi of Lemberg from 1843 to 1848. In September 1848, Kohn's family was poisoned, and both he and his infant daughter Teresa were killed. The prime suspect was an Orthodox Jew.

90. Bernard (Dov) Hausner (1874–1938), Orthodox rabbi, military chaplain, Zionist activist, and representative of Lemberg Jewry to Russian occupation authorities during the war. Hausner would have been forty years old at the time he met An-sky.

91. Theodor Herzl (1860–1904), Jewish writer from the Habsburg Empire, who founded the political Zionist movement in the late 1890s, and developed a large following among Galician Jews.

92. Refers to the series of trials held in Paris from 1894 to 1899 in which French Jewish military officer Alfred Dreyfus (1859–1935) was wrongfully convicted of treason. Due to the outburst of antisemitic hostility that erupted in France during the trial, Herzl despaired of the possibility that Jews could successfully integrate into European society and began to advocate for the exodus of Jews from Europe, and the creation of a Jewish state.

93. Moritz (Moses) Güdemann (1835–1918), chief rabbi of Vienna (1891–1918) who initially supported Herzl's efforts to establish a secular Jewish state, but ultimately rejected the Zionist movement as antithetical to Judaism.

94. Tsadok ha-Kohen (Tsadok Rabinowitz) (1823–1900), prominent leader of the Izhbitser Hasidic sect in Lublin.

95. A play in German and Hebrew on Tsadok-Cohen's name, meaning "He's no *tsadik* (righteous man)."

96. Mathias Acher (born Nathan Birnbaum) (1864–1937), Jewish writer and activist from Vienna who championed a wide range of causes including Zionism, Diaspora Nationalism, Yiddish cultural nationalism, and religious Orthodoxy.

97. Chaim Zhitlowsky (1865–1943), Russian-Jewish writer, a founding figure of Diaspora Yiddish nationalist ideology, and An-sky's closest lifelong friend.

98. Hebrew, *Shabbes Teshuvah*, observed on the Sabbath that falls during the ten days between Rosh Hashanah and Yom Kippur.

99. Hebrew, judge; a communal figure who held the authority to decide cases of personal or business conflicts according to Jewish law.

100. Dębica is located about 210 kilometers (130 miles) east of Lvov.

101. Nikolai Iudovich Ivanov (1851–1919), general and chief of staff for the Russian Army's Southwestern Front (July 1914–March 1916).

102. Nikolai Vladimirovich Ruzskii (1854–1918), general and commander of Russia's Third Army in Galicia (July 1914–September 1914); chief of staff for the Northwestern and Northern Fronts (September 1914–1917).

103. Russian, a Cossack village or unit within a Cossack military settlement typically found in the south Russian Empire.

104. Zholkva (Ukrainian, Zhovkva; Polish, Żółkiew): 1910 population: 9,463 (Jewish population: 3,845, or 40.6%); 1921 population: 7,867 (Jewish population: 3,718, or 47.3%).

105. Rava-Ruska: 1910 population: 10,775 (Jewish population: 6,112, or 56.7%); 1921 population: 8,970 (Jewish population: 5,048, or 56.3%).

106. Two versts is about 2 kilometers, or 1.24 miles.

107. Hebrew, the third and final set of daily prayers in the Jewish liturgy, recited at sunset or nightfall.

108. The San River was regarded as a natural dividing line between eastern and western Galicia.

109. Rzeszów: 1910 population: 23,688 (Jewish population: 8,785, or 37.1%); 1921 population: 24,942 (Jewish population: 11,361, or 45.5%).

110. Hebrew, a quorum of ten men that is the minimum number required for public prayer.

111. Tarnów: 1910 population: 36,731 (Jewish population: 5,108, or 41.2%); 1921 population: 35,347 (Jewish population: 15,608, or 44.2%).

112. Seven or eight versts is about five miles.

113. Demidov was forty-one years old at the time.

114. Four or 5 versts is about 2.5 to 3 miles.

115. See note 105.

116. The date was likely August 31, 1914. The Battle of Rava-Ruska, between the Russian Third Army and Austro-Hungarian Fourth Army, took place during the last week of August 1914.

117. Russian, "*Vashe blagorodie*," a term of address to officers of rank up to and including that of captain.

118. Radko-Dmitriev (1859–1918), Bulgarian-born lieutenant general in the Russian Army; commander of the Russian Third Army in Galicia (April 1915–June 1915).

119. Hebrew, ritual bath, immersion in which is thought to bestow a state of ritual purity on the individual; it is typically used by Jewish women after menstruation and childbirth, and by some men before daily prayers and certain holidays.

120. An-sky was born Shloyme-Zanvl Rapoport and took "An-sky" as his literary pseudonym in the early 1890s.

121. Part of the old Russian system of measurement, equivalent to 2.13 meters, or 7 feet; 5 sazhen is about 35 feet.

122. Polish, Falcons, an athletic association that promoted militant Polish nationalism founded in Lemberg in 1867.

123. May refer to Avram Iakovlevich Garkavi (Harkavy) (1835–1919), Russian-Jewish historian, public activist, and head of the Oriental manuscripts division at the Imperial Public Library (1876–1919).

124. Russian, *Rech*, daily newspaper and the main organ of the liberal Constitutional Democrat (Kadet) Party, of which Demidov was a member.

125. Tuchów: about 18 kilometers (11 miles) south of Tarnów; 1910 population: 2,667 (Jewish population: 455, or 17%).

126. Flying Columns were widely used mobile medical units in Russia during the war.

127. Mikhail Dmitrievich Nechvolodov (1867–1951), commander of the 175th Baturin Regiment (*Pekhotnyi Baturinskii polk*), 1914–1916.

128. Yiddish, (from Hebrew, *tallit*), a four-cornered prayer shawl worn during morning prayers.

129. Hebrew, phylacteries made of small leather boxes, containing parchments inscribed with verses from the Torah, attached to the forearm and forehead with leather straps, usually worn during morning prayers.

130. Hebrew, booths; the name of the Jewish autumnal festival that begins five days after Yom Kippur.

131. Hebrew, teacher in a heder, or Jewish primary school sustained by community funds and usually attended by children of poor families.

132. One verst is about 0.62 miles.

133. The main character in Tolstoy's 1886 short story "How Much Land Does a Man Need?" about an ambitious peasant who pursues increasing amounts of land.

134. Pavel Dmitrievich Dolgorukov (1866–1927), Russian liberal politician and manager of a Red Cross unit in Galicia (1914–1915).

135. On February 8, 1915, the Russian Twentieth Army Corps surrendered to the German Tenth Army in what became known as the Second Battle of the Masurian Lakes.

136. Eighteen versts is about eleven miles.

137. About 64 to 85 meters, or 210 to 280 feet.

138. Pilzno: 1910 population: 2,367 (Jewish population: 820, or 35%); 1921 population: 3,546 (Jewish population: 752, or 21%).

139. Aleksandr Ivanov Zvegintsev (1869–1915), Russian Army colonel, geographer, and Octobrist Party politician.

140. Hebrew, East, an image placed on the eastern wall of a home or synagogue as a reminder that one should direct their prayers toward Jerusalem.

141. Twenty versts is about 12.4 miles.

142. German, doctor's assistant, higher in rank than a medical student but unqualified to serve as a doctor.

143. Fyodor Fydorovich Trepov (1854–1938), Russian Army general; served as military governor-general during the second Russian occupation of Galicia and Bukovina (October 1916–March 1917); a member of the nationalistic and antisemitic Black Hundreds group.

144. Pavel Grigorievich Kurlov (1860–1923), Russian Army general and statesman.

145. Refers to the Kiev division of EKOPO.

146. David Semyonovich Margolin (1850–1918), prominent Russian-Jewish industrialist, public activist, and patron from Kiev.

147. Members of the Union of Russian People (*Soiuza russkogo naroda*), a Russian nationalist party founded in 1905.

148. The trial of Menachem Mendel Beilis (1874–1934), a Jewish factory owner from Kiev accused of committing ritual murder in March 1911. Beilis was acquitted of the murder charge in October 1913. An-sky attended the trial and published articles about it in the Russian newspaper *Rech* (Speech) and the Yiddish newspaper *Lodzher Tageblat* (Łódź Daily).

149. Aleksei Semyonovich Shmakov (1852–1916), Russian lawyer, prosecutor at the Beilis trial, Duma deputy, widely known as an antisemite.

150. Georgii Georgievich Zamyslvoskii (1872–1920), Russian lawyer, prosecutor at the Beilis trial, Duma deputy.

151. Anastasia Nikolaevna Chebotarevskaia (1876–1921), Russian modernist writer, critic, translator, wife of Fyodor Sologub.

152. Officially known as the League to Fight against Antisemitism (*Liga bor'by s antisemitizmom*), founded in Petrograd by Maksim Gorky, Leonid Andreev, and Fyodor Sologub in early 1915.

153. Russian, *Politicheskii biuro*, or Politbiuro, was a forum for Jewish political and cultural leaders, established in St. Petersburg in 1905.

154. Ivan Logginovich Goremykin (1839–1917), Russian minister of the Interior (1895–1899) and chairman of the Council of Ministers (1906, 1914–1916), known for his conservative, loyalist views.

155. George Buchanan (1854–1924), British ambassador to Russia (1910–1917).

156. Aron Fishilev Perelman (1876–1954), Russian-Jewish cultural activist and owner of the Brockhaus Efron publishing house.

157. Pavel Nikolaevich Miliukov (1859–1943), Russian politician, founder, and leader of the liberal Constitutional Democrat (Kadet) Party (1905–1917); foreign minister of the Provisional Government (March–May 1917).

158. Sergei Dmitrievich Sazonov (1860–1927), Russian foreign minister (1910–1916).

159. Aleksei Aleksandrovich Goldenveiser (1890–1979), Russian-Jewish lawyer, publicist, and liberal activist from Kiev.

160. Grand Duke Mikhail Aleksandrovich (1878–1918), Russian major-general and commander of the Caucasian Native Cavalry (the "Wild Division"); the youngest brother of Tsar Nicholas II.

161. Tadeusz Rutowski (1852–1918), Polish president of Lvov's City Council during the first Russian occupation of Galicia (1914–1915), and a writer, publicist, and patron of the arts.

162. John Sobieski (1629–1696), was King John III of Poland and Grand Duke of Lithuania (1674–1696).

163. Refers to St. Lawrence Church, a seventeenth-century Roman Catholic church.

164. Turkish wind instrument used to play folk music in the Caucuses and Middle East regions.

165. Aleksandr Modestovich Khiriakov (1863–1940), Russian prose writer, literary critic, and Tolstoy scholar.

166. Stryi (Polish, Stryj): 1910 population: 30,942 (Jewish population: 10,718, or 34.6%); 1921 population: 27,358 (Jewish population: 10,988, or 40.2%).

167. An-sky uses the term *uezd* (in Russian, district) here; under Habsburg administration, the town of Stryi was defined as both a district (*bezirk*) and the center of Stryi region (*kreis*).

168. Thirty to 40 versts is about 18.6 to 25 miles.

169. German, unit of currency used in the Austro-Hungarian Empire.

170. Hebrew, books of rabbinic exegesis on parts of the Hebrew Bible.

171. Rodion Anatolievich Bonch-Osmolovskii (1884–1938), Russian agricultural economist, Union of Zemstvos member, and Socialist Revolutionary activist.

172. A medical society founded in 1885 and named for Nikolai Ivanovich Pirogov (1810–1881), a prominent Russian scientist and field surgeon.

173. Founded in 1765 in St. Petersburg; primarily dedicated to advancing agricultural production in the Russian Empire.

174. Count Vladimir Alekseevich Bobrinskii (1868–1927), Russian deputy to the Second, Third, and Fourth Dumas; scion of an old noble family.

175. Hebrew, Hope of Zion.

176. Hebrew, Hand of the Diligent.

177. "Jargon" was a disparaging term for Yiddish language in Eastern Europe.

178. Avraam-Alfred Goratsievich Gintsburg (1865–1936), a gold mining magnate who was commissioned at age fifty-one as a lieutenant during the war; the fifth eldest son of Baron Goratsii Evzelevich Gintsburg (1833–1909).

179. Lubaczów (Ukrainian, Liubachiv): 1910 population: 6,444 (Jewish population: 2,171, or 33.7%); 1921 population: 5,303 (Jewish population: 1,715, or 32.3%).

2. FALL 1915

1. Aleksandr Nikolaevich Volzhin (1860–1933), Russian statesman, director of the Department of General Affairs for the Ministry of Internal Affairs (July 1914–September 30, 1915).

2. Aleksandr Goratsievich Gintsburg (1863–1948), Russian-Jewish gold mining magnate, the second oldest son of Baron Goratsii Evzelevich Gintsburg (1833–1909).

3. Mark Abramovich Varshavskii (1844–1922), Russian-Jewish industrialist, patron, and public activist, and president of the St. Petersburg/Petrograd Jewish Community (1910–1918).

4. Prince Nikolai Borisovich Shcherbatov (1868–1948), Russian liberal politician, minister of Internal Affairs (June 5, 1915–September 26, 1915).

5. K. V. Nikolaevskii, Socialist Revolutionary activist and ethnographer of Russian peasant life.

6. Russian, *Novoe vremia*, a popular liberal paper published in St. Petersburg (1868–1917).

7. Sergei (Israel) Lazarevich Tsinberg (1873–1939), Russian-Jewish literary historian; he later composed an important eight-volume history of Jewish literature, between 1929 and 1937.

8. Refers to Jewish volunteer battalions in the British Army, founded by Vladimir Jabotinsky and Joseph Trumpeldor, with the goal to help liberate Palestine from Ottoman rule. The corps was organized in Egypt in February 1915 among refugees from Palestine.

9. Semyon Afanasievich Vengerov (1855–1920), Russian literary historian, philologist, and bibliographer.

10. Fyodor Dmitrievich Batiushkov (1857–1920), Russian philologist, theater and literary critic, director of St. Petersburg's court theaters before 1917.

11. Semyon Solomonovich Iushkevich (1868–1927), Russian-Jewish realist prose writer and dramatist.

12. Published in three volumes as *Russkaia literatura XX veka, 1890–1910* [Twentieth century Russian literature, 1890–1910], ed. S. A. Vengerov, A. G. Fomin, and E. V. Anichkov, 3 vols. (Moscow: Mir, 1914–1917). An-sky's biography appeared in the third volume.

13. David Iakovlevich Aizman (1869–1922), Russian-Jewish prose writer and dramatist.

14. Leonid Ivanovich Lutugin (1864–1915), Russian geologist and liberal activist.

15. Shmaryahu Levin (1867–1935), Russian-Jewish liberal politician and Zionist leader.

16. A division among Jews in ancient Israel: the Cohen belonged to the tribe of priests who performed the most important sacred rituals; Levites performed other rites of worship; all other Jews were considered Israelites.

17. Yiddish, brain, also as in intellect or mind.

18. Vladimir (Ze'ev) Jabotinsky (1880–1940), Russian-Jewish writer, translator, and Zionist leader and theorist; he organized the Zion Mule Corps (later known as the Jewish Legion) during World War I and founded the Revisionist Zionist movement in the interwar period.

19. At the start of World War I, the World Zionist Organization moved its headquarters from Berlin to neutral Copenhagen in order to continue its worldwide activities.

20. Aryeh Babkov (1881–1948), Russian-Jewish Zionist activist and author.

21. Cultural Zionist group, founded in St. Petersburg in 1912.

22. Samuil Moiseevich Shryro, Russian-Jewish oil magnate and patron of Jewish culture and political activism, including An-sky's prewar ethnographic work.

23. A Russified Hebrew term, meaning a student of a yeshivah, or academy for advanced Torah study for young Jewish men.

24. Refers to a speech given before the State Duma by Naftali Markovich Fridman (1863–1921), a Jewish Kadet from Kovno Province to the Third and Fourth State Dumas. The full text of Fridman's speech, in which he openly discussed the expulsions and hostage-taking of Jews by the Russian military, was published in the Russian liberal press (*Rech'*, August 3, 1915).

25. Count Pavel Nikolaevich Ignatiev (1870–1945), Russian minister of National Education (January 1915–December 1916).

26. In mid-August 1915, the Tsar's Council of Ministers issued a circular that allowed for the provisional expansion of the borders of the Pale, which granted Jews permission to settle in the towns and cities of the Russian interior, with the exception of the Moscow, Petrograd, and Cossack regions.

27. Avraham Menakhem Mendel Ussishkin (1863–1941), Russian-Jewish Zionist activist; he later became a prominent Labor Zionist leader in mandate Palestine and Israel.

28. Nikolai Nikolaevich Khodotov (1878–1929), Russian actor at the Aleksandrinskii Theater in Petrograd.

29. Aleksandr Akimovich Sanin (1869–1956), Russian actor, drama instructor, and director at the Moscow Free Theater (1914–1919), which was sponsored by the patron V. P. Sukhodolskii.

30. Efim (Yekhiel) Vladimirovich Chlenov (1863–1918), Russian Zionist leader and author.

31. Prince Nikolai Leonidovich Obolensky (1878–1960), Russian politician and member of the Ministry of Internal Affairs.

32. Andrei Ivanovich Shingaryov (1869–1918), Russian liberal politician and physician.

33. Leopold Antonovich Sulerzhitskii (1872–1916), Polish-born director, painter, and educator associated with the Moscow Art Theater.

34. Emmanuil (Mendel) Lvovich Gurevich (1866–1952), Russian-Jewish author, translator, and Social Democrat; his pseudonyms included E. Stirnov, V. Danevich, and K. Petrov.

35. Aleksei Vasilievich Peshekhonov (1867–1933), Russian economist, journalist, and founder of the Popular Socialist Party (*Narodno-Sotsialicheskaia Partiia*) (1906–1922).

36. Refers to the Jewish Historical-Ethnographic Society (*Evreiskoe istoriko-etnograficheskoe obshchestvo*).

37. Refers to the Jewish Literary Society, founded in St. Petersburg in 1907 as a division of the Society for the Promotion of Culture among Jews of Russia (*Obshchestva dlia Rasprostraneniia Prosveshcheniia Mezhdu Evreiami v Rossii*, or OPE).

38. "Activism" was a term that Vladimir Jabotinsky used in his wartime writings to denote militant Zionist activism and specifically the aims of the Jewish legion.

39. SS refers to the Union of Socialist Revolutionaries (Russian, *Soiuz sotsialistov-revoliutionerov*); KS: Peasant Alliance (Russian, *Krest'ianskii soiuz*); Bundists: members of the General Jewish Workers' Union (Yiddish, *Algemeyner Yidisher Arbeter Bund*).

40. Israel Isidor Eliashev (1873–1924), Russian-Jewish critic and historian of Yiddish classical literature, better known by his pseudonym, Baal-Makhshoves (Hebrew, The Thinker).

41. Shmuel Niger (Charney) (1883–1955), Russian-Jewish scholar of Yiddish literature, language, and folklore; in 1919, he emigrated from Russia to the United States.

42. Gabriele D'Annunzio (1863–1938), Italian writer, poet, and nationalist politician.

43. George Bernard Shaw (1856–1950), Irish writer and socialist activist in England.

44. Edgar Wallace (1875–1932), English crime writer and journalist.

45. Russian, Truth; a Russian political newspaper founded in 1903 in Moscow; in 1912, it became the official organ of the Russian Social Democratic Labor Party.

46. Founded by Gorky in Petrograd, in operation 1915–1918.

47. An-sky wrote this essay in Russian in December 1914; its title was "The Book of Signs (A Jewish Apocalypse)" (*Kniga znamenii* [*Evreiskii apokalipsis*]).

48. Russian, *Sovremennik*, an important Russian thick journal founded by the poet Aleksandr Pushkin in 1836.

49. Kuzhi (Lithuanian, Kuršėnai; Yiddish, Kurshan); Orany (Lithuanian, Varėna): during the Great Retreat in spring 1915, the Russian Army High Command claimed that Jews in these towns were sheltering German soldiers; the accusations were proven to be false but the army nonetheless burned these towns and expelled their Jewish residents.

50. Lev Moiseevich Aizenberg (1867–195?), Russian-Jewish lawyer, publicist, and expert on Jewish rights of residence in the Russian Empire.

51. Sergei Efimovich Kryzhanovskii (1862–1935), assistant minister of the Interior (1906–1911), imperial secretary, and member of the State Council.

52. Aleksei Nikolaevich Khvostov (1872–1918), Russian statesman, politician, and minister of the Interior (September 26, 1915–March 3, 1916); a staunch conservative and antisemite.

53. Nikolai Pavlovich Muratov (1867–19?), governor of Tambov and Kursk Provinces (1906–1915), member of the Ministry of Internal Affairs (1915); known for reactionary policies, he was closely allied with the antisemitic conservative A. N. Khvostov (see note 52).

54. Arkadii Georgievich Gornfeld (1867–1941), Russian-Jewish essayist, literary critic, and translator.

55. Viktor Vasilievich Muizhel (1880–1924), Russian Populist prose writer.

56. Venedikt Aleksandrovich Miakotin (1867–1937), Russian historian and Populist politician.

57. Russian, *Russkoe slovo*, liberal newspaper published in Moscow.

58. Russian, *Birzhevie vedomosti*, liberal newspaper published in St. Petersburg.

59. Aleksandr Abramovich Kipen (1870–1938), Russian-Jewish Populist prose writer.

60. Zinovy Isaevich Grzhebin (1869–1929), Russian art collector, patron, editor, and publisher.

61. Nikolai Vasilievich Drizen (1868–1935), Russian theater historian and censor of theatrical works.

62. Aleksandr Dmitrievich Samarin (1868–1932), chief procurator of the highest governing body of the Russian Orthodox Church, the Most Holy Synod (July 1915–September 1915); he was a zemstvo leader in Moscow and head of the Russian Red Cross during the war.

63. Varnava (Vasilii Aleksandrovich Nakropin) (1859–1924), Russian Orthodox Bishop.

64. About 117 kilometers (73 miles).

65. Meir Kreinin (1866–1939), Russian-Jewish industrialist, vice chairman for the Society for the Promotion of Culture among Jews of Russia (OPE) and cofounder with Simon Dubnov of the autonomist Folkspartey in 1907.

66. Yitzhok Grinboym (1879–1970), Polish-Jewish writer and Zionist activist from Warsaw; he later became the state of Israel's first Interior minister (1948–1949).

67. A meeting of the two unions was held in Moscow, September 7–9, 1915.

68. Prince Georgii Evgenievich Lvov (1861–1925), Russian liberal statesman, chairman of the Union of Zemstvos (1914–1917); he later served as the first prime minister of the Provisional Government (March–July 1917).

69. Mikhail Vasilievich Chelnokov (1863–1935), Russian industrialist, Kadet deputy to the Duma, chairman of the Union of Towns, and mayor of Moscow (1914–1917).

70. Dmitrii Leonovich Rubinshtein (1876–1937), Russian-Jewish banker, Mason, and Kadet Party activist.

71. See note 6.

72. Lev Moiseevich Kliachko (Lvov) (1873–1939), Russian-Jewish journalist; as chairman of the Committee of Journalists at the State Council, he had close ties to many public activists, ministers, and government circles.

73. Stepan Petrovich Beletskii (1873–1918), Russian statesman, director of the Department of Police (1912–1914).

74. Nikolai Aleksandrovich Berdiaev (1874–1948), Russian religious and political philosopher.

75. Russian, *Shchit*, an anthology of philosemitic articles published in 1916 in Moscow and edited by Sologub, Gorky, and Leonid Andreev. It included articles by leading Russian intellectuals.

76. Iosif Vladimirovich Gessen (1865–1943), Russian-Jewish liberal politician, legal expert, and editor of the Kadet newspaper *Rech'* until 1917.

77. Dmitrii Vladimirovich Filosofov (1872–1940), Russian literary art critic and religious writer.

78. Dmitrii Sergeevich Merezhkovskii (1866–1941), Russian writer, religious philosopher, and critic.

79. Naum Lvovich Aronson (1873–1943), Russian-Jewish sculptor.

80. Russian, *Melkii bes*, a 1905 novella by F. K. Sologub, whose main character Peredonov is morally corrupt, paranoid, and eventually loses his sanity.

81. Russian, *Russkoe bogatstvo*, a monthly thick journal founded in St. Petersburg in 1879.

82. French, series of public lectures or performances scheduled on a similar day of each month.

83. Nikolai Sergeevich Rusanov (1859–1939), Russian Socialist Revolutionary activist and writer.

84. Stepan Semyonovich Kondrushkin (1873–1919), Russian war correspondent and essayist.

85. Count Illarion Ivanovich Voronstov-Dashkov (1837–1916), lieutenant-general in the Russian Army and commander of the Caucasian Front (1905–August 1915).

86. Vladimir Fyodorovich Dzhunkovskii (1865–1938), Russian governor-general of Moscow (1908–1913); first deputy Interior minister (1913–August 1915). He issued a report in June 1915 about Rasputin's drunken behavior at a Moscow restaurant.

87. Russian, *Starinnye teatr*. Founded by Drizen and N. N. Evreinova in 1907 in St. Petersburg; it staged adaptations of medieval and early modern French, German, Spanish, and Italian literary works.

88. Refers to the Progressive Bloc (*Progressivnyi blok*), a coalition of moderate conservatives and liberals in the State Duma formed in August 1915 and led by P. N. Miliukov, which called for a government of "public confidence" and improved management of Russia's war effort.

89. Pyotr Lvovich Bark (1869–1937), Russian statesman and minister of Finance (1914–1917).

90. Refers to the Jewish People's Group (*Evreiskaia narodnaia gruppa*), a political party founded in 1907 in St. Petersburg to fight for civil rights for Jews.

91. Aleksandr Alekseevich Khvostov (1857–1922), Russian minister of Justice (July 1915–July 1916), and uncle of the conservative Minister of Interior Affairs Aleksei Nikolaevich Khvostov (see note 52).

92. Aleksander Vasilievich Krivoshein (1857–1921), Russian minister of Agriculture (1908–1915).

93. Anatolii Fyodorovich Koni (1844–1927), Russian jurist, academician at the Petersburg Academy of Sciences, member of the State Council of the Russian Empire (1907–1917).

94. Ioanna (Anna, or Hannah) Markovna Jabotinskaia (1884–1949), Russian-Jewish Zionist editor and activist, and Vladimir Jabotinsky's wife (1907–1940).

95. Aleksandr Rafailovich Kugel (1864–1928), Russian-Jewish theater critic and director of the experimental Distorting Mirror Theater (*Teatr krivoe zerkalo*) in St. Petersburg (1908–1928).

96. Abram Rekhtman (1890–1972), Russian-Jewish folklorist and Yiddish writer; he traveled with An-sky during the pre-war Ethnographic Expedition, and published his memoirs of the expedition in 1958.

97. Solomon Borisovich Iudovin (1892–1954), Russian-Jewish graphic artist, known for his wood engravings that portrayed revolutionary motifs and Jewish shtetl life; together with Abram Rekhtman he accompanied An-sky during the Ethnographic Expedition.

98. Likely refers to Solomon Gepshtein (1882–1961), Russian-Jewish Zionist author and publicist.

99. Mikhail Vasilievich Alekseev (1857–1918), Russian Army General; commander of the Southwestern and Northwestern Fronts (1914–1915).

100. Moisei Lvovich Trivus (Shmi) (1865–?): Russian-Jewish liberal politician and author.

101. Russian, *Evreiskaia nedelia*; a Russian-language Jewish weekly paper, published in Moscow under that title after April 1915 and before then as *Novyi voskhod* (New Dawn).

102. Formally known as the Jewish Society for the Promotion of the Arts (*Evreiskogo obshchestva pooshchreniia khudozhestv*), founded in Petrograd in 1915.

103. Ilia Iakovlevich Gintsburg (1859–1939), Russian-Jewish sculptor and founder of the Jewish Society for the Promotion of the Arts (see note 102).

104. John Henry Patterson (1867–1947), Irish-born lieutenant colonel in the British Army who commanded the Zion Mule Corps (1915) and Jewish Legion (1917–1918) in combat against Ottoman forces.

105. Refers to the Battle of Gallipoli (or Gallipoli Campaign), failed British military campaign against the Ottoman Empire (April 1915–January 1916) to seize the sea route along the Dardanelle Straits leading to Istanbul, in which the Zion Mule Corps fought under Patterson's command.

106. Iosif (Joseph) Trumpeldor (1880–1920), highly decorated Russian-Jewish veteran of the Russian Army who immigrated to Palestine in 1911; in February 1915, he cofounded with Vlaimir Jabotinsky the Zion Mule Corps among Jewish war refugees in Alexandria.

107. In mid-October 1915, Great Britain offered to give Cyprus to Greece, with the condition that Greece enter the war on the side of the British. Greece rejected the offer.

108. Mikhail Isaakovich Sheftel (1862–1919), Russian-Jewish lawyer, leading figure in the Society for the Promotion of Enlightenment among Jews in Russia (OPE).

109. Moisei Lvovich Maimon (1860–1924), Russian-Jewish portrait painter.

110. Maksimilian Grigorievich Syrkin (1858–after 1928), Russian-Jewish lawyer and art historian, former editor of the Russian-Jewish weekly papers *Voskhod* and *Novyi voskhod*.

111. The play was published in Russian under Sologub's name as *Kamen', broshennyi v vodu (Semia Vorontsovykh)* in fall 1915.

Index

Acher, Mathias [Nathan Birnbaum], 74, 172n96

Aizenberg, Lev Moiseevich, 143–144, 147, 153, 178n50

Aizman, David Iakovlevich, 134, 176n13

Alekseev, Mikhail Vasilievich, 153, 163n38, 181n99

American Jewish Joint Distribution Committee, 11, 31

Andreev, Leonid Nikolaevich, 43, 110, 115, 139, 168n22

Aronson, Naum Lvovich, 149, 157–158, 180n79

Babkov, Aryeh, 135, 177n20

Bark, Pyotr Lvovich, 152, 180n89

Baron, Salo, 26

Batiushkov, Fyodor Dmitrievich, 133, 176n10

Beilis, Menachem Mendel, 109, 174n148

Beletskii, Stepan Petrovich, 148, 153, 180n73

Berdiaev, Nikolai Aleksandrovich, 148, 180n74

Betzalel, 135, 141

Bialik, Chaim Nachman, 7

Bikerman, Iosif Menassievich, 43, 167n18

Bobrinskaia, Sofia Alekseevna, 82, 94

Bobrinskii, Georgii Aleksandrovich, 18, 22, 61, 106–108, 112–113, 170n63

Bobrinskii, Vladimir Alekseevich, 122, 175n174

Bonch-Osmolovskii, Rodion Anatolievich, 122, 124, 175n171

Bramson, Leontii Moiseevich, 14, 43, 154–155, 167n16

Braudo, Aleksandr Isaevich, 43, 167n17

Brody, 16, 23–24, 50–51, 60–61, 64–69, 102, 169n53

Brusilovskii, 43

Buchanan, George, 174n155

Buczacz, 31, 74

Bukovina, 1, 3, 12, 28

Burdzhalov, Georgii Sergeevich, 45, 168n32

Bykhovskii, Grigorii Borisovich, 46, 108, 169n45

Cahan, Abraham, 32

Chebotarevskaia, Anastasia Nikolaevna, 110, 148–150, 154, 158, 174n151

Chelnokov, Mikhail Vasilievich, 147, 152, 179n69

Chlenov, Efim (Yekhiel) Vladimirovich, 138, 177n30

D'Annunzio, Gabriele, 142, 178n42

Dębica, 75, 81–82, 86, 94, 172n100

Demidov, Igor Platonovich, 15, 16, 41, 42, 82–83, 86–87, 90, 97, 99–100, 104, 167n8

Demidov, Lev Platonovich, 43, 111, 167n9

Demidova, Ekaterina Iurievna, 91–92, 94, 95

Diamand, Herman, 18–19, 24, 69–72, 114–116, 121–123, 170n77

Dinezon, Yankev, 5

Dolgorukov, Pavel Dmitrievich, 97–99, 101, 104, 106, 173n134

Dreyfus, Alfred, 72, 171n92

Drizen, Nikolai Vasilievich, 144, 147, 151–152, 154, 157, 179n61

Dubno, 58–60

Dubnov, Simon, 7, 31, 160n11

Duker, Abraham, 33

Dzhunkovskii, Vladimir Fyodorovich, 150–151, 180n86

Eikhe, 70

EKOPO (Jewish Committee for the Aid of War Victims), 1, 11, 14, 18, 30, 31, 32, 43, 44, 111, 116, 122, 140, 151, 155

Eliashev, Israel, 141, 178n40

Evlogii Georgievskii, 22, 68, 106, 170n74

Fainberg, David Fadeevich, 18, 61, 69, 72, 170n62

Filosofov, Dmitrii Vladimirovich, 149, 180n77

Franz Joseph, 72, 169n56, 171n88

Free Economic Society, 122, 175n173

Fridman, Naftali Markovich, 108, 136, 177n24

Ganeizer, Evgenii Adolfovich, 45, 168n36

Gepner, Iulii Grigorievich, 46, 169n46

Gepshtein, Solomon, 153, 181n98

Gessen, Iosif Vladimirovich, 148–149, 180n76

Gintsburg, Aleksandr Goratsievich, 129, 134, 148, 154, 156–158, 176n2

Gintsburg, Alfred Goratsievich, 124–125, 175n178

Gintsburg, Ilia Iakovlevich, 156–158, 181n103

Gintsburg, Vladimir Goratsievich, 46, 124, 169n48

Ginzburg, Moisei Akimovich, 48, 169n50

Goldenveizer, Aleksei Aleksandrovich, 111–112, 175n159

Goremykin, Ivan Logginovich, 110, 152, 174n154

Gorky, Maksim, 29, 43, 110, 129, 141–143, 148, 152, 168n21

Gornfeld, Arkadii Georgievich, 144, 154, 179n54

Grinboym, Yitzhok, 146, 179n66

Grzhebin, Zinovy Isaevich, 144, 147, 151, 179n60

Güdemann, Moritz, 72, 171n93

Gurevich, Sasha Viktorovna, 137

Gurevich, Sofia Sergeevna, 151

Gurevich-Stirnov, Emmanuil Lvovich, 139, 178n34

Harkavy, Avram Iakovlevich, 90, 173n123

Hausner, Bernard, 18–19, 31, 72–75, 106–108, 112–116, 121–123, 163n39, 171n90

Herzl, Theodor, 72, 84, 171n91

Ianushkevich, Nikolai Nikolaevich, 12, 18, 76, 162n27, 164n46

Idelson, Avram Davidovich, 44, 168n29

Ignatiev, Pavel Nikolaevich, 137, 177n25

Iudovin, Solomon Borisovich, 153, 181n97

Iushkevich, Semyon Solomonovich, 133–134, 139, 176n11

Ivanov, Nikolai Iudovich, 14, 24, 76, 110–111, 172n101

Jabotinskaia, Ioanna Markovna, 153, 157, 181n94

Jabotinsky, Vladimir (Ze'ev), 29, 135–136, 138, 141–142, 147, 157, 176n8, 177n18

Jarosław, 78, 86, 102

Jewish Ethnographic Expedition, 4, 60

Jewish Historical-Ethnographic Society, 4, 7, 28, 30, 32, 44, 140

Jewish Legion, 29, 133, 135–136, 138, 141–142, 146–147, 176n8, 181n105
Jewish Literary Society, 140, 142, 145, 178n37
Jewish Pale of Settlement, 4, 10, 28
Jewish People's Group, 152
Jewish Political Bureau, 110, 136–137, 143, 152, 154–156, 174n153
Jewish Society for the Promotion of the Arts, 30, 156–158, 181n102
Johnson, Ivan Vasilievich [Ivanov], 45, 139, 168n33

Khiriakov, Aleksandr Modestovich, 115, 175n165
Khodotov, Nikolai Nikolaevich, 138–139, 177n28
Khvostov, Aleksandr Alekseevich, 153, 181n91
Khvostov, Aleksei Nikolaevich, 144, 150, 152–154, 156, 179n52
Kiev, 14, 16, 46–47, 108, 111–112
Kipen, Aleksandr Abramovich, 144, 179n59
Kliachko, Lev Moiseevich, 148, 180n72
Kohn, Abraham, 72, 171n89
Kondrushkin, Stepan Semyonovich, 150, 180n84
Koni, Anatolii Fyodorovich, 153, 181n93
Kovno, 149–150, 154
Kreinin, Meir, 145, 151–153, 179n65
Krivoshein, Aleksander Vasilievich, 153, 181n92
Kruk, Herman, 33
Kryzhanovskii, Sergei Efimovich, 144, 179n51
Kugel, Aleksandr Rafailovich, 153, 181n95
Kurlov, Pavel Grigorievich, 108, 174n144
Kuzhi, 143, 178n49

Lander, F. E., 69, 113–114, 120, 123–124, 170n78
Lenin, V. I., 7

Levin, Shmaryahu, 134, 176n15
Lubaczów, 27, 126–127, 176n179
Lutugin, Leonid Ivanovich, 134, 176n14
Lvov, 16, 18, 22, 24, 62–64, 69–76, 106–108, 112–116, 170n76
Lvov, Georgii Evgenievich, 147, 163n38, 179n68

Maimon, Moisei Lvovich, 157, 182n109
Makhover, I. M., 46, 169n43
Margolin, David Semyonovich, 108, 110–111, 174n146
Mazor, Moisei Saveliev, 46, 169n42
Merezhkovskii, Dmitrii Sergeevich, 149, 180n78
Mess, Samuil, 48–49, 67
Miakotin, Venedikt Aleksandrovich, 144, 179n56
Mikhail Aleksandrovich, 112, 175n160
Miliukov, Pavel Nikolaevich, 30, 110, 175n157, 180n88
Minsk, 14, 145
Moscow, 14, 16, 42–43, 44–45, 111, 138–140
Muizhel, Viktor Vasilievich, 144, 179n55
Muratov, Nikolai Pavlovich, 144, 179n53

Naidich, Yitzhak Asher, 15, 28, 41, 42, 44, 111, 143, 147–148, 167n3
Nechvolodov, Mikhail Dmitrievich, 92, 173n127
Neitel, Yaakov Lvovich, 147
Nemirovich-Danchenko, Vladimir Ivanovich, 43, 45, 144, 167n14
Niger, Shmuel, 141, 178n41
Nikolaevskii, K. V., 129, 176n5
Nikolai Nikolaevich, 12, 42, 150, 164n46, 167n6

Obolensky, Nikolai Leonidovich, 138, 177n31
Oleszyce, 77–78
Orany, 143, 178n49

Ordynskii, Sergei Pavlovich, 45, 82, 168n34

Patterson, John Henry, 157, 181n104
Perelman, Aron Fishilev, 110, 174n156
Peretz, I. L., 5
Peshekhonov, Aleksei Vasilievich, 140, 146, 151, 178n35
Petrograd (St. Petersburg), 4, 10, 12, 14, 16, 27–30, 43–44, 109–110, 129–138, 140–158
Pilzno, 103–104, 174n138
Pirogov Society, 122, 124, 175n172
Popov, Nikolai Aleksandrovich, 43, 45, 167n13
Pozner, Solomon Vladimirovich, 43, 110–111, 143, 148, 152, 167n19

Radivilov, 16, 21, 24, 47–50, 169n49
Radko-Dmitriev, 86, 173n118
Rasputin, 145, 147, 149–151
Ratner, B. E., 16–17, 43, 45–47, 49–50, 52, 54–55, 60, 69, 74, 84–85, 88, 167n10
Rava-Ruska, 77, 85, 89, 105, 172n105
Red Cross, 14, 19
Rekhtman, Abram, 153, 181n96
Rennenkampf, Paul von, 42, 76, 167n7
Rovno, 15, 39–41, 166n1
Rozov, Izrail Anshelovich, 44, 168n28
Rubinshtein, Dmitrii Leonovich, 148, 179n70
Rusanov, Nikolai Sergeevich, 150, 180n83
Rutowski, Tadeusz, 113, 175n161
Ruzskii, Nikolai Vladimirovich, 76, 153, 172n102
Rzeszów, 27, 34, 78–80, 172n109

Samarin, Aleksandr Dmitrievich, 145, 147, 179n62
Sanin, Aleksandr Akimovich, 138–139, 177n29
Sazonov, Sergei Dmitrievich, 110, 152, 175n158

Seredina Buda, 45
Shabad, Tsemakh, 32, 69, 84, 171n79
Shapiro, Maria L., 84, 89–90, 102
Shaw, George Bernard, 142, 178n43
Shcherbatov, Nikolai Borisovich, 28, 129, 136–137, 143–144, 146–147, 176n4
Sheftel, Mikhail Isaakovich, 157, 182n108
Sheremetev, Sergei Vladimirovich, 69–70, 171n80
Shingaryov, Andrei Ivanovich, 138, 177n32
Shmakov, Aleksei Semyonovich, 109, 174n149
Shryro, Samuil Moiseevich, 135–137, 177n22
Sliozberg, Genrikh Borisovich, 14, 28, 30, 129, 133, 137, 143, 148, 156, 168n26
Smorgon, 145–146, 156
Sobiesky, John, 113–114, 175n162
Sologub, Fyodor Kuzmich, 29, 30, 43, 109–110, 148–150, 154, 158, 168n23
Stryi, 18, 21, 27, 116–121, 175n166
Sulerzhitskii, Leopold Antonovich, 139, 149, 178n33
Syrkin, Maksimilian Grigorievich, 157–158, 182n110
Syrkin, Naum Solomonovich, 46, 169n44

Tarnów, 15, 26, 42, 82–91, 97–103, 172n111
Tolstoy, L. N., 81
Trakhtman, Lev Borisovich, 91, 94, 96
Trepov, Fyodor Fydorovich, 108, 174n143
Trivus, Moisei Lvovich, 156, 181n100
Trumpeldor, Joseph, 157, 176n8, 182n106
Tsadok ha-Kohen, 74, 171n94
Tsinberg, Sergei (Israel) Lazarevich, 133, 141–142, 152, 176n7
Tuchów, 25, 88, 91–94, 173n125

Union of Towns (VSG), 14–15, 16, 45, 49, 89, 100, 106, 146, 152
Union of Zemstvos (VZS), 14–15, 61, 64, 84, 144, 146, 152
Ussishkin, Avraham, 138, 177n27

Varnava (Vasilii Aleksandrovich
Nakropin), 145, 147, 179n63
Varshavskii, Mark Abramovich, 28, 129,
133–136, 138, 140, 143, 148, 154, 156–157,
176n3
Vengerov, Semyon Afanasievich, 133–134,
176n9
Vilna, 7, 32–33
Vinaver, Maksim Moiseevich, 44, 152, 156,
168n27
Volfson, Raisa Iakovna, 84, 99–100
Volzhin, Aleksandr Nikolaevich, 129,
176n1

Vorontsov-Dashkov, Illarion Ivanovich,
150, 180n85

Wallace, Edgar, 142, 178n44
Warsaw, 12, 15, 33, 43
Wygodski, Jacob, 32

Zamyslovskii, Georgii Georgievich, 109,
174n150
Zhitlowsky, Chaim, 33, 74, 172n97
Zholkva, 23, 77, 113–114, 123–124, 172n104
Żółkiewsky, 113
Zveginstev, Aleksandr Ivanov, 103, 174n139

S. A. An-sky, pseudonym of Shloyme-Zanvl Rapoport (1863–1920), was a Russian Jewish writer, ethnographer, and cultural and political activist. He is best known today for his play *The Dybbuk*.

Polly Zavadivker is Assistant Professor of History and Director of the Jewish Studies Program at the University of Delaware.